Children's Play
**Research Developments and
Practical Applications**

Special Aspects of Education

A series of books edited by Roy Evans, Roehampton Institute, London, UK, and Herman Green, Northern Illinois University, De Kalb, Illinois, USA.

ISSN: 0731-8413

Children's Play
Research Developments and
Practical Applications

Edited by
PETER K. SMITH
University of Sheffield

GORDON AND BREACH SCIENCE PUBLISHERS
New York   London   Paris   Montreux   Tokyo

Previously published as Vol. 19 Nos. 1 and 2 of *Early Childhood Development and Care.*

Gordon and Breach Science Publishers

P.O. Box 786
Cooper Station
New York NY 10276
United States of America

P.O. Box 197
London WC2E 9PX
England

58, rue Lhomond
75005 Paris
France

P.O. Box 161
1820 Montreux 2
Switzerland

14-19 Okubo 3-chome,
Shinjuku-ku,
Tokyo 160
Japan

Library of Congress Cataloging in Publication Data

Main entry under title

Children's Play
    (Special aspects of education, ISSN 0731-8413; v. 6)
    Previously published as vol. 19 nos. 1 and 2 of
Early childhood development and care.
    1. Play—Addresses, essays, lectures.   2. Child
development—Addresses, essays, lectures.   I. Smith,
Peter K.   II. Early childhood development and care.
III. Series.
HQ782.C45 1985   155.4′18   85-24864
ISBN 0-677-20000-5 (pbk)
ISBN 0-677-21390-5 (hbk)

Contents

Introduction to the Series

Increasingly in the last 10 to 15 years the published literature within the field of care education has become more specialised and focussed: an inevitable consequence of the information explosion and the wider scope of theoretical and practical knowledge being required of students in both the traditional and developing areas of professional training. Students within initial and post-initial training evidently need to have ready access to specialised theoretical and pedagogical resources relevant to the context of their future professional involvements which also develop special aspects of an area of study in a critically evaluative way.

In the study of education and pedagogy, the analytical and experimental approaches of psychology, philosophy, sociology, social anthropology, etc., have provided insights into teaching and learning, into schooling and education. Historically these disciplines have focussed their attention on relatively homogeneous populations. Increased worldwide mobility has created a need for a more pluralistic approach to education—particularly in Western countries—and a more broadly based concern for educational issues related to particular contexts. Hence, further literature has developed in recent years which is concerned with the pedagogical and curricular issues raised, for example, in connection with the "urban school", minority ethnic groups, disadvantaged and handicapped groups, and children who live apart from their families.

What is frequently missing from discipline-orientated studies is a real appreciation of context beyond the "general". What is often not present in the contextual study is an interdisciplinary analysis of the issue that provides a framework for practice.

The present series—"Special Aspects of Education"—is

intended to bridge the gap between the problems of practice, as perceived in a variety of contexts, and theory, as derived from a variety of disciplines. Books accepted or commissioned for inclusion in the series will manifestly be expected to acknowledge the interdisciplinary nature of the issues and problems in the field of education and care and, addressing themselves to particular contexts, to provide a conceptual framework for identifying and meeting special educational needs.

ROY EVANS
HERMAN GREEN

Play research and its applications:
A current perspective

PETER K. SMITH
University of Sheffield

AFTER SOME decades in the doldrums, there have been exciting developments in play research in the last ten years. New methodologies and ideas are being used and debated. The applied benefits of play are being considered in more thorough and systematic ways. Hopefully, we can still value the fun and enjoyment of play while taking a more balanced and objective view of what play is, what its benefits are, and the role of play in development, education, training, therapy and recreation.

Some principal publications of the last five years will indicate the spate of current play research. Rubin (1980) edited an excellent short collection which overviewed play research with children. Fagen (1981) brought out an exhaustive and surely classic account of animal play behaviour, and Smith (1982 and Commentary) discussed the links between animal and human play. Pepler and Rubin (1982) edited an interesting and argumentative series of articles on children's play, and Rubin, Fein and Vandenberg (1983) provide a very thorough review of the whole topic. Schaefer and O'Connor (1983) edited a comprehensive sourcebook of research and practice with play therapy. Three edited collections have appeared last year. Smith (1984) covers animal and human play from a variety of perspectives. Yawkey and Pellegrini (1984) consider both developmental and applied aspects of children's play. Bretherton (1984) focusses on symbolic play, the most prototypical example of children's play.

In this book, all the articles are about play in young children. They review recent research, mention salient problems, and discuss the application of our knowledge of play in several areas of professional practice.

ANIMAL PLAY

Play has its origins in the warm-blooded animals—the birds and mammals. Although play has now been described in a number of bird species, it is not nearly as frequent or obvious as it is in many mammals. Almost every reader will recall seeing lambs gambolling, kittens stalking, chasing and pouncing, and similar forms of exuberantly active play in puppies, calves, and the young of many other domestic and wild species.

The similarities of the play of other mammals to that of humans are limited, but worth some brief discussion. Firstly, such play is characteristic of young mammals—not the very young, helpless infants, rather young who are independently mobile but have not yet reached sexual maturity. Secondly, it is usually argued that because play is common in mammalian species, and quite frequent in occurrence for a certain period of the lifespan, then it must have some particular advantages or benefits for the young animal. This is especially so because play has some disadvantages; the young animal uses up energy, and is in greater risk of danger from accidents or from predators, if it is playing rather than just resting, for example.

A lot of benefits have been proposed for mammalian play. The most common are that it serves as exercise and physical training to enhance physical development; that it practises skills, such as fighting and hunting, in a safe, 'playful' way when serious practice would be dangerous; that it enhances social bonding between the young in a litter or a social group; that it helps an individual learn its position in a social group; and that it facilitates creative or innovative learning (this last argument has been especially advanced for play in monkeys and apes).

These possible benefits are not mutually exclusive; in any particular species, it is quite conceivable that play could have several of the above benefits. Also, benefits might vary with the particular type of play. Most mammalian play involves general locomotor activity (e.g. gambolling), or non-serious fighting and chasing involving special signals such as a play-face, or play-gambol. In the monkeys and apes, play with objects is also fairly frequently seen.

Actual firm evidence that play has these benefits is, however, hard to come by. One possibility is that, while playful behaviour can have a number of benefits such as those suggested, play is not essential for these benefits; play might be just one way of getting them. This is a very important distinction. If play is essential for some purpose, such as social bonding for example, the failure to play could be disastrous. However if play is one means of social bonding (others being e.g. grooming, sleeping in the same place, sharing food), then a failure to play could be compensated for.

These issues are currently under active debate by ethologists studying animal play. The reader can consult Fagen (1981) and Smith (1982, 1984) for recent in-depth reviews, and Martin and Caro (1985) for the argument that the essential function of animal play may have been overstated. Many aspects of this debate have correspondences in recent research in children's play.

CHILDREN'S PLAY

Both animal play and human play have been studied a great deal since the turn of the century. Karl Groos assembled an impressive amount of observation, theory and speculation in his two volumes, *The Play of Animals* (1898) and *The Play of Man* (1901). In the latter, he takes the term play in a very broad sense, to include also adult games, rituals and competitions. However most subsequent researchers (at least those in a psychological tradition) have tended to restrict play to the characteristic forms seen in young children, especially from the preschool years up to puberty.

The forms of play, and characteristic use of play materials in young children, were documented by child psychologists in the USA, Britain, Germany and elsewhere in the 1920's and 1930's. However it was the work of Jean Piaget in the next few decades, and especially his book *Play, Dreams and Imitation in Childhood* (1951, first published in French in 1945) which provided a framework for studying infant and child development and an influential approach to defining and categorising play.

In this book, as in others, Piaget described detailed daily observations he made on the behaviour of his own three children. For example, at 15 months he described the beginnings of pretend play in his daughter, Jacqueline, when she would lie down on a cloth, or a rubber donkey's tail, put her thumb in her mouth, and blink her eyes; she would grin as well, apparently pretending to 'go to sleep'. Such clearly playful examples don't occur until the second year of life. Before then, and indeed through to the pre-school years of the 3 and 4 year old, infants engage in a lot of exploratory learning, especially using their eyes (visual exploration) and their hands (manipulative exploration). Recent research on these developments is summarised by Fenson and Schell in this volume. They discuss the early kinds of exploratory behaviour, and the stages in development of pretend play from 12 to 36 months of age. By the preschool years, though not before, exploration and play have become fairly clearly separable sorts of behaviour.

Piaget (1951) summarised three stages in the development of play—sensorimotor or practice, pretend or symbolic, and games with rules. Sensorimotor or practice play refers to the sort of exploratory learning or practice behaviours that are especially seen in the young infant, though they continue beyond. Pretend or symbolic play, most common from 2 to 6 years, is the prototypical example of children's play. Observers generally agree that it is definitely play, and Piaget's writings, in due course, helped focus considerable research attention on it. Games with rules, characteristic of 6 or 7 years onwards, have some agreed structure which a participant is normally constrained to follow. In this respect it differs from a common view of play as being unconstrained by rules. Whatever the merits or not of this latter position, Piaget's framework helped to separate the research on children's play from that on games, the latter following rather separate traditions (see for example, Sutton-Smith and Roberts, 1981).

Most of Piaget's observations were of pretend play with objects, such as dolls, combs, etc. He did not pay much attention to rough-and-tumble play, or indeed to the social nature of play generally. Rough-and-tumble play, or play fighting and chasing, is quite common in preschool children and through up to adolescence. Probably its developmental impact is more social than cognitive. It's primarily a friendly activity, accompanied by laughter, and children tend to choose their friends to play-fight with; though there are some indications that toward adolescence, elements of dominance or actual aggression may also enter into play-fights. Teachers and supervisors seem to have a rather ambivalent attitude towards rough-and-tumble. A book on the topic has been published by Aldis (1975), and a recent summary is available in Humphreys and Smith (1984).

Another area neglected by researchers in the Piagetian tradition was language play. Yet, children play with words, and the meanings of words, just as they do with objects and other actions. Psychologists devoted a lot of attention to child language from the 1960's on. Language play was well documented in a book by Weir (1962), who recorded the talk of her 2-year-old son at night, in his crib; but further research on language play was slow to get off the ground. Recent work is reviewed by Kuczaj in his book (1983), and his chapter in this volume.

Piaget wrote about play within his own theoretical framework. In this, he saw the child's activity at any particular time as being somewhere between the poles of assimilation, and accommodation. Assimilation refers to the child using already known skills or schemas in a situation, while accommodation refers to the child having to try out new skills or schemas in order to achieve some end-result or goal. Piaget saw pretend play as being largely or entirely assimilative; for example, a child pretending to bake cakes could just take some wooden blocks, put them in a box and take them out, 'baked', a few moments later. Actually baking cakes would be accommodative for a preschool child, who would be faced with having to mix the pastry, leave it in the oven until ready, and then taste the results!

Piaget thought that a lot of constructive activity in young children, such as building with blocks, and making models, was somewhere between assimilation and accommodation, and therefore somewhere between play and work. There is some end-point or goal, but the child can change the goal in the course of the activity (perhaps deciding to make something easier) so the constraints are not as great as in a work-like situation.

Nevertheless activities such as building with blocks are usually called play. Indeed an Israeli psychologist, Sara Smilansky, put forward a scheme in which constructive play appeared as an intermediate stage between functional or practice play, and symbolic play. This scheme has been used by a number of researchers. A critique of this scheme is presented in the chapter by Smith, Takhvar, Gore and Vollstedt (this volume). This chapter also reviews the ways in which play in children is defined, and some problems in the observation of play behaviour.

The problem of defining what we mean by play is important when the layperson's use of the term may not coincide with its use by psychologists. We have just mentioned Piaget's position on constructive 'play' as an example. Other examples are provided by the new technology of computers and video games which children are so fascinated by, even as early as the preschool years. Do children 'play' with video games? What do children do if they are left to 'play' with a microcomputer? The latter issue is considered by Simon (this volume), while a good introduction to the general area of children's use of video games and computers is in the book by Greenfield (1984).

APPLICATIONS OF PLAY

The most obvious and basic value of play, is that children enjoy it. Indeed, enjoyment or positive affect enters into most of the current definitions of play. Anyone who recalls their own childhood playing, or who watches children chasing or pretending, will see it as something pleasurable in it's own right, usually with no harmful consequences to self or others; and this in itself should be sufficient justification for putting a high value on play.

Nevertheless it is, and has been, necessary to stress the value of play because adequate facilities for children's play are not always available. Not all homes are well equipped with things children are allowed to play with, or with companions, or with plentiful indoor and outdoor space for playing. Play groups and nurseries can provide these, but can cater for only a minority of the age group and for restricted periods. Modern cities and housing estates commonly lack suitable outdoor areas for children to play in. It is ironic that the desirability of another restaurant or cinema is rarely questioned, although these are used by adults more for enjoyment than for any very basic needs. Yet, although children's play areas (if well designed) can be enjoyed by children just as much as a restaurant (if well designed) can be enjoyed by adults, it is often the case that some extra justification seems to be needed for devoting facilities to children's play; presumably because no financial gain is forthcoming. As a result it seems at times as though we are excessively puritanical in our approach to children's play, seeking to establish strong benefits for learning or socialization when simple harmless enjoyment is surely sufficient rationale.

Of course, play equipment does need to be well designed, and play areas well equipped and laid out. In part, this is a matter of choosing suitable materials to provide sufficient variety and challenge for the kinds of children concerned. Age is a major factor, but, for example, the special needs of handicapped children may suggest special kinds of toy or play area design. These are discussed in the chapter by McConkey (this volume), and briefly by Naylor (this volume) in mentioning Wolff's (1979) work on playgrounds for blind children.

Naylor also points out the important consideration of safety in designing play equipment. While play is normally harmless, any challenging play will involve some risks. These cannot be eliminated completely, but careful design can greatly reduce the chances that any harm will come to a child through playing.

PLAY, EDUCATION AND LEARNING

The trend in attitudes to play through the twentieth century has so far been one of increasing acceptance that it is important for cognitive, social and emotional development. In the nineteenth century, views were varied. Herbert Spencer (1898) saw play as a "tendency to superfluous and useless exercise of faculties that have been quiescent", and a number of writers saw the wilder aspects of play and games as something that needed control and socialisation by adults. However by the 1930s and 1940s play was widely seen in a much more favourable light. Susan Isaacs (1929) stressed both the educational and emotional value of children's play, and this has been echoed by theorists such as Vygotsky,

Singer, Smilansky and Bruner, who see play as a means of furthering cognitive skills and creativity. Many preschool educational curricula put a high value on free play activities.

Not all educationists and theorists have taken this line. For example Maria Montessori, one of the pioneers of the modern nursery school, valued constructive activities such as colour and shape matching much above fantasy or pretend play. Something of this attitude follows through into Piaget's theorising, discussed above. Piaget was influenced by Montessori's thinking, and he too saw accommodative or constructive activities as more cognitively valuable than assimilative activities, including pretend play. However Piaget did see a value for free play in the consolidation of skills, and also for the child's developing confidence in his or her activities.

Despite the more cautious view of Piaget, the 'textbook' view of play has become that it is unquestionably important if not essential for children's learning. Indeed, Piaget is often reinterpreted as supporting this latter view. Observations of what goes on in play does suggest that much learning of various kinds is likely to take place: exploratory learning of new materials, learning of social roles and negotiations in sociodramatic play, creative learning in trying out new possibilities free of external constraints.

One practical application of this view has been the encouragement of 'play tutoring' in nursery schools and kindergartens. This is adult encouragement of sociodramatic play, pioneered by Smilansky (1968) in Israeli preschools. Sociodramatic play, involving role play by several players (e.g. in spacemen and monsters; doctors, nurses and patients; or parents and baby) is perhaps the most complex form of play seen in preschool children. Some children do a lot of it, but others, more likely it seems from disadvantaged backgrounds, do much less. Many studies of play tutoring have found that it can assist not only the development of this form of play in children, but also their cognitive and language skills as well.

The methods of play tutoring or training are reviewed by Christie (this volume). As he points out, it does promote cognitive growth, but the reasons are not yet wholly clear. The cognitive benefits may be due as much to the extra adult interaction involved, as to the actual symbolic or pretend nature of the play. These theoretical issues are further discussed in Smith and Syddall (1978), Brainerd (1982), Saltz and Brodie (1982) and Christie and Johnsen (1985).

There have been other studies on the cognitive benefits of play. A number have used laboratory situations, in which children are given periods of some ten minutes either for free play with objects, or for some training or control experience, to see whether free play acts as a facilitator of problem solving or creativity. Early examples were an associative fluency task by Dansky and Silverman (1973), and a lure retrieval experiment by Sylva (1977). However these studies have been plagued either by unimpressive results, or by problems of experimenter effects and inadequate control groups. At present, the evidence from quite a large number of such studies remains equivocal, and it may be that the artificial nature of laboratory studies, and the short time intervals involved, are not appropriate for detecting whatever effects play does have. The issues are reviewed further in Smith and Simon (1984).

More naturalistic environments for considering the role of play in learning are discussed by Simon (this volume) in connection with computers and LOGO, and by McConkey (this volume) in connection with the play of handicapped children. In both these cases however, the role of adults is important in guiding or structuring the child's activities at crucial points. The role of the adult is clearly a vital one in evaluating the role of play in learning. The more that adults intervene, the more the context of the behaviour is likely to change from one of play to one of instruction or work.

Nevertheless, if the intrinsic motivation and enjoyment of play can be combined with the advantages of adult involvement, this may provide some very suitable contexts for cognitive growth. This is the thinking behind the play tutoring or training programmes (Christie, this volume), and of structuring play in the early years at school (Manning and Sharp, 1977).

So far as free play is concerned, the possibility must be faced that it may not be as essential for cognitive growth as some previous writers have suggested. Certainly, we don't yet have evidence to strongly support the link. As was discussed earlier in connection with play in mammals, it may be that free play in children does bring about situations in which learning occurs, but that such learning can also occur in non-play contexts. Thus, play may not be as uniquely important as is sometimes assumed, at least in educational terms. This however is a conclusion which is still very much a controversial one. Many writers and researchers would still feel that play can nurture a child's imaginative potential, even if the methods of assessment used in research so far have failed to prove this conclusively. The processes of 'imaginative' and sociodramatic play bear many similarities to the processes of later creative abilities, such as story writing (Cowie, 1984).

PLAY AND SOCIAL AND EMOTIONAL DEVELOPMENT

One area where free play may come into its own is in social development with peers, and emotional security. Although adults can help foster peer relationships, and indeed even implement social skills training programmes to help children who find it difficult to make friends (see Wanlass and Prinz, 1982, for a review), by and large it is a defensible view that much peer socialisation has to be worked out by children themselves, and free play is a very obvious way to do this, especially for young children. It's difficult to cite much firm evidence one way or the other. However, the increased sociodramatic play brought about by play tutoring programmes seems to have its most distinctive impact on social development, such as social participation (Smith, Dalgleish and Herzmark, 1981; Rubin, Fein and Vandenberg, 1983).

Free play, especially with the traditional 'messy' or expressive materials such as water, sand, clay, and paints, seems also to be calming for children and may help them acquire self-confidence and a sense of mastery over materials. Such a view is consistent with Piaget's position, as these assimilative activities enable a child to express him- or herself in varied ways using known skills and without risk of failure or censure. Such experiences may be especially important for handicapped children (McConkey, this volume). Another important area of application is for children in hospital (see Lindquist, Lind and Harvey, 1977, or Bolig, 1984). Research is limited, but some case studies suggest that play can reduce anxiety in children who are hospitalised and thus under stress both from the new environment and from separation from parents and family.

A specialised application of free play is play therapy with disturbed children. Here, expressive and symbolic play materials are used both for diagnostic purposes, to assist the therapist in understanding the child's problems and needs, and for therapeutic purposes, as a means of anxiety reduction and cathartic release of tension. There are many schools of play therapy, and many apparently successful case studies, though at present research studies on the relative efficacy of the different methods of therapy, and of alternatives to play therapy, are not very numerous or well-controlled. A well-known case study of play therapy is provided by Axline's (1976) book, *Dibs: In Search of Self*. The area is reviewed by Schaefer (this volume), and a comprehensive reference source is Schaefer and O'Connor (1983).

SUMMARY

Most of the research on the functions of children's play over the last couple of decades has concentrated on cognitive growth and creativity as important outcomes. Yet it is certainly arguable that the social and emotional benefits of free play are likely to be as important, if not more so. This could be a useful research impetus in the future. It would be helpful to know more about whether or how play reduces anxiety, or has therapeutic value, and whether certain forms of play provide particularly useful experience and opportunity for social skills and friendship formation.

Previous and future research will be especially valuable in the applications of play: the optimal design of play environments, and the use of play in applied settings such as schools, hospitals and clinics. Basic research is also necessary to clarify further the normative course of play development and the most useful ways of defining and measuring play. However the bedrock of our attitude to play, I believe, should be its intrinsic pleasure and enjoyment. Research should only enhance, and not detract from, this very rewarding and fascinating activity.

References

Aldis, O. (1975). *Play Fighting*. New York: Academic Press.

Axline, V. (1976). *Dibs: In search of self*. Harmondsworth: Penguin.

Bolig, R. (1984). Play in hospital settings. In T.D. Yawkey and A.D. Pellegrini (eds), *Child's Play: Developmental and applied*. Hillsdale, N.J.: Erlbaum.

Brainerd, C.J. (1982). Effects of group and individualized dramatic play training on cognitive development. In D.J. Pepler and K.H. Rubin (eds), *The Play of Children: Current theory and research*. Basel: Karger.

Bretherton, I. (ed.) (1984). *Symbolic Play: The development of social understanding*. New York: Academic Press.

Christie, J.F. and Johnsen, E.P. (1985). Questioning the results of play training research. *Educational Psychologist*, **20**, 7-11.

Cowie, H. (ed.) (1984). *The Development of Children's Imaginative Writing*. London: Croom Helm.

Dansky, J.L. and Silverman, I.W. (1973). Effects of play on associative fluency in pre-school-aged children. *Developmental Psychology*, **9**, 38-43.

Fagen, R. (1981). *Animal Play Behavior*. New York: Oxford University Press.

Greenfield, P.M. (1984). *Mind and Media*. London: Fontana.

Groos, K. (1898). *The Play of Animals*. New York: Appleton.

Groos, K. (1901). *The Play of Man*. London: William Heinemann.

Humphreys, A.P. and Smith, P.K.. (1984). Rough-and-tumble in preschool and playground. In P.K. Smith (ed.), *Play in Animals and Humans*. Oxford: Basil Blackwell.

Isaacs, S. (1929). *The Nursery Years*. London: Routledge & Kegan Paul.

Kuczaj, S.A. II. (1983). *Crib Speech and Language Play*. New York: Springer.

Lindquist, I., Lind, J. and Harvey, D. (1977). Play in hospital. In B. Tizard and D. Harvey (eds), *Biology of Play*. London: SIMP/Heinemann.

Manning, K. and Sharp, A. (1977). *Structuring Play in the Early Years at School*. London: Ward Lock Educational.

Martin, P. and Caro, T.M. (1985). On the functions of play and its role in behavioral development. *Advances in the Study of Behavior*, **15**, 59-103.

Pepler, D.J. and Rubin, K.H. (eds) (1982). *The Play of Children: Current theory and research*. Basel: Karger.

Piaget, J. (1951). *Play, Dreams and Imitation in Childhood*. London: Routledge & Kegan Paul.

Rubin, K.H. (ed.) (1980). *Children's Play*. San Francisco: Jossey-Bass.

Rubin, K.H., Fein, G.G. and Vandenberg, B. (1983). Play. In P.H. Mussen and E.M. Hetherington (eds), *Handbook of Child Psychology (4th edn)*, Vol 4. New York and Chichester: Wiley.

Saltz, E. and Brodie, J. (1982). Pretend-play training in childhood: A review and critique. In D.J. Pepler and K.H. Rubin (eds), *The Play of Children: Current theory and research*. Basel: Karger.

Schaefer, C.E. and O'Connor, K.J. (eds) (1983). *Handbook of Play Therapy*. New York and Chichester: Wiley.

Smilansky, S. (1968). *The Effects of Sociodramatic Play on Disadvantaged Preschool Children*. New York: Wiley.

Smith, P.K. (1982). Does play matter? Functional and evolutionary aspects of animal and human play. *Behavioral and Brain Sciences*, **5**, 139-84.

Smith, P.K. (ed.) (1984). *Play in Animals and Humans*. Oxford: Basil Blackwell.

Smith, P.K., Dalgleish, M. and Herzmark, G. (1981). A Comparison of the effects of fantasy play tutoring and skills tutoring in nursery classes. *International Journal of Behavioral Development*, **4**, 421-41.

Smith, P.K. and Simon, T. (1984). Object play, problem-solving and creativity in children. In P.K. Smith (ed.), *Play in Animals and Humans*. Oxford: Basil Blackwell.

Smith, P.K. and Syddall, S. (1978). Play and non-play tutoring in preschool children: Is it play or tutoring which matters? *British Journal of Educational Psychology*, **48**, 315-25.

Spencer, H. (1898). The principles of psychology, Vol.II, pt.2. New York: Appleton.

Sutton-Smith, B. and Roberts, J. (1981). Play, games and sports. In M.C. Triandis and A. Heron (eds), *Handbook of Cross-cultural Psychology: Developmental Psychology*, Vol.4. Boston: Allyn and Bacon.

Sylva, K. (1977). Play and learning. In B. Tizard and D. Harvey (eds), *Biology of Play*. London: SIMP/Heinemann.
Wanlass, R.L. and Prinz, R.J. (1982). Methodological issues in conceptualizing and treating childhood social isolation. *Psychological Bulletin*, **92**, 39-55.
Weir, R. (1962). *Language in the Crib*. The Hague: Mouton.
Wolff, P.M. (1979). The adventure playground as a therapeutic environment. In D. Canter and S. Canter (eds), *Designing for Therapeutic Environments: A review of research*. New York and Chichester: Wiley.
Yawkey, T.D. and Pellegrini, A.D. (eds) (1984). *Child's Play: Developmental and applied*. Hillsdale, N.J.: Erlbaum.

The origins of exploratory play

LARRY FENSON and ROBERT E. SCHELL

San Diego State University

NEWBORN babies enter the world with a range of reflexive behaviors, such as orienting, sucking, and startle responses. But they have no knowledge of the world they encounter. It is largely through their playful transactions with people and objects that they gain information about physical and social aspects of their environment. At first, these transactions are mainly visual, due to infants' inability to control their hands and fingers. However, by about 5 months of age, infants gain the ability to retrieve objects within their reach. At that point, manipulative investigation begins to combine with visual exploration, vastly enhancing their range of sensorimotor experiences.

By the end of the first year of life, young children have made impressive strides in understanding the nature of the world. Now, through the medium of pretend play, they also begin to simulate features of their own experience in order to further explore the relation between themselves and other people and objects in their environment. The onset of pretend play, however, by no means signals the end of visual exploration and manipulative investigation. Each of these three types of inquiry continues to contribute important input to children's ever-changing conceptions of their world. To understand the contributions of each of these types of inquiry, researchers have found it convenient to look at each type in relative isolation.

Thus, we consider, in turn, developmental changes in visual exploration, manipulative investigation, and pretend play. The reader, however, should remember that, while we can break these behaviors apart for purposes of discussion, they generally are linked together in the playing child.

Before proceeding, a word is in order concerning terminology. Some writers have made a hard distinction between investigatory behaviors, directed toward the extraction of information from the environment and play, whose purpose seems to be the creation of variation in the environment (Berlyne, 1960). Though this distinction has proven useful both theoretically (Wohlwill, 1984) and empirically with children of preschool age and older (Hutt, 1970), the distinction is very difficult to maintain with infants and toddlers. In their manipulative activities, children often seem intent on exploiting the feedback properties of objects or in creating change through their actions. Conversely, children's pretend activities often seem designed to explore social relationships. Hence, we do not strictly adhere to this distinction in the present paper. Rather, we prefer Henderson's (1984) term "exploratory play."

VISUAL EXPLORATION

Infants are visually responsive to their environment from the moment of birth. Over the course of infancy, they acquire a great deal of information about the world solely through visual exploration of their surroundings. Research on changing patterns of visual attention has, moreover, been unusually fruitful in informing us about changes with age in infants' abilities to process and remember information. In this section, we describe how the visual events which attract and maintain infants' attention change with age, and consider what these changes tell us about their cognitive development.

Birth to six months

Newborn babies spend only about 5% of their waking time looking at the world about them (White, 1971). They are most likely to be visually attracted to stimuli showing high rates of change, e.g., moving objects, pulsating lights, and bold patterns with vivid light-dark contrast, such as a large black triangle on a white background (Haith, 1966).

By just over 2 months of age, infants spend about 35% of their time observing their visual environment. High rate of change continues to be a potent elicitor at this point (as at all ages), but improved scanning and tracking abilities now enable infants to notice and inspect more subtle aspects of visual events, such as the amount of complexity or detail in a pattern. In additon, the visual interest of infants begins to reflect cumulative effects of their experience, so that novel objects are distinguished from familiar ones and are preferred. Cohen, Gelber, and Lazar (1971), for example, found that infants become bored with successive presentations of a simple geometric form, but show renewed interest when a different pattern is shown. Moreover, they found that infants look longer at the new pattern if it differs from the old pattern in both form and color than if it varies in only one of these dimensions.

As their neurological development continues and infants gain further visual experience, they begin to construct some fundamental schemes or concepts. A schema for human beings, for example, is probably one of the first to develop. It is perhaps for this reason that the 4-month-old will look more at a two- or three-dimensional representation of a human face than at any other pattern that is comparable in complexity, brightness, and other potent factors that elicit attentiveness. In addition, most babies not only are attracted to the human face, but they spend considerable time systematically inspecting it (Hainline, 1978; Kagan, 1967).

Six to twelve months

Visual exploration of the environment continues to be an apparent source of pleasure and a vehicle for learning from 6 to 12 months of age as infants show interest in increasingly complex and novel patterns. Thus, as experience accumulates and memory improves from the more limited skills of the 2- to 4-month-old to the better recall capacities of the older infant, infants' concepts become more firmly established. This enables the infant, for example, to distinguish not only between human and nonhuman forms, but also between mother and other people (see Sherrod, 1981).

An increased ability to recall more fully and precisely what has been experienced before also enables infants to notice and study departures from the normal arrangement of features in a pattern. For example, by 6–9 months of age, infants will usually show heightened interest in a known schema in which the features have been rearranged. Detection of this type of discrepancy or incongruity may occur even prior to 6 months of age for especially well-established schemes, such as a human face (Caron, Caron, Caldwell, and Weiss, 1973).

Infants are particularly likely to show sustained interest in patterns and events which are moderately rather than extremely discrepant from their prior experience. This makes sense. A scrambled face, for example, which preserves a sufficient number of recognizable features to permit association with the face schema would require more processing time than that required to identify a normal face and would therefore likely command the infant's attention for a relatively longer period of time. However, a face so rearranged that it could no longer be identified would probably hold little interest for the infant and receive minimal attention (Kagan, Kearsley, and Zelazo, 1978).

Twelve to thirty-six months

Infants are quite efficient information processors by 12 months of age. They need attend for only a few seconds to something that might have occupied their attention for 20 seconds or more a half-year earlier. Typically, their looking-time decreases steadily to successive presentations of a familiar visual pattern, but each new pattern generates renewed visual interest. At the same time, most 12-month-olds continue to prefer complex patterns over simple ones and to prefer meaningful subjects to abstract patterns (Fenson, Sapper, and Minner, 1974).

Few investigators have studied the determinants of visual attentiveness beyond the first year. Jerome Kagan's work is an exception. In two major longitudinal studies, Kagan and his colleagues (Kagan, 1971; Kagan et al., 1978) measured the visual responsiveness of young children, at various points in time from 3 to 30 months of age, to normal and discrepant events. In one episode, Kagan and his coworkers showed the children three dimensional clay heads with normal, rearranged, or missing features. In another episode, the children looked at slides, some slides showing ordinary subjects (e.g., girl, cat), others showing an incongruous scene (e.g., a fully-dressed girl in a bathtub, a giant cat, a man with four arms). In still another episode, the children watched a series of trials in which a small car rolled down a ramp and knocked over a form made of colored balls. After a set number of these trials, a pin was inserted so that the form would no longer fall over when hit by the car.

In general, Kagan and his colleagues found that infants were very attentive to such episodes at 4 or 5 months, but their interest dropped sharply at 7–9 months, and then increased again at 13 or 20 months of age. In addition, for some events, the children's attention increased even further in the third year (at 27 or 30 months). Kagan suggests that infants show a drop in attention at 7-9 months because they more rapidly assimilate the information contained in the event. The increase in children's attentiveness to discrepant events in the second and third years, Kagan suggests, is due to the children's increasing ability to not only detect transformations, but to generate questions and hypotheses about them. For example, a child might not only ask, "What happened to the eyes" but go on to generate one or more answers to the question.

By the middle of the second year then, it seems quite clear that symbolic competencies begin to play a prominent role in infants' visual exploration. And, as we discuss in the following sections, it is the infants' symbolic competencies that begin to regulate other forms of their exploratory play as well.

MANIPULATIVE EXPLORATION

Physical contact with objects enables the infant to acquire many types of information about objects not available by visual inspection alone. When infants handle objects, of course, they also are likely to experience new forms of visual input. They see objects in motion and in changing positions, in each case, as a result of their *own* actions. This combination of visual and manual exploration makes an inestimable contribution to infants' developing conceptions of the world. In this section, we describe some of the changes that occur in infants' manipulative exploration over the early years of life and discuss how manipulative exploration and cognitive development influence one another.

Birth to six months

During the first few months of life, manipulative exploration is quite limited. During this time, babies do watch their own hand movements, but they cannot coordinate their hands and eyes, and are unable to reach out and retrieve things. On the other hand, from the earliest days of life, infants will grasp objects pressed into their palms and will watch the object as it comes within their field of vision. And, long before the sixth month, infants learn to bring objects within their grasp into their field of vision and to their mouth, generating another mode of exploration—oral investigation.

Although manual skill is quite limited during these first 5–6 months of life, infants will use whatever means are available to create or maintain interesting events. For example, infants will kick on a foot pedal or suck at a rapid rate on a specially constructed pacifier (Siqueland and Delucia, 1969) in order to produce an interesting visual display. As suggested some time ago by Papousek (1967), moreover, young infants may respond to produce even relatively uninteresting contingent events, simply for the opportunity to exercise control over the environment. Of course, infants' delight in controlling the environment is also reflected in their participation in early social games such as peekaboo (Watson, 1972).

Piaget (1962) found a developmental pattern in these early "stimulus-seeking" actions by infants. He called them circular reactions to emphasize the way that infants repeat an action over and over. The earliest circular reactions are those which are repeated for their own sake, essentially exercise of a bodily motion in which the action is not a means to an end but an end in itself. These "primary circular reactions" occur in the earliest months of life.

By 4 months of age, children begin to display "secondary circular reactions." These are behaviors in which the child repeats an action in order to produce an interesting effect external to the child's own body. For example, when one of the senior author's sons was about 4 months old, he would often fret when lying in his crib for no apparent reason other than boredom. He did not yet have the manual skill to play with objects. So an interesting mobile was suspended above his crib and a string was tied from the mobile to his ankle. By kicking, he could produce a colorful display of moving, jingling forms, which delighted and fascinated him for long periods of time (sometimes up to an hour). Within a few weeks, he became more proficient, having learned to bring about the maximum effect with minimal foot motion.

Some months later, children learn to alter their responses in order to vary the effect in some way. Piaget termed these more systematic mini-experiments "tertiary circular reactions."

Six to twelve months

From 6 months of age on, with mastery of visually guided manual activity, manipulative exploration expands rapidly. Paralleling visual exploration, novel objects are selected and explored to a greater extent than familiar ones, at least by 9 months. Interestingly, although infants will show more initial and sustained interest in a novel object at 9 months of age, they also may inhibit reaching for a novel object by this age, taking time first to examine the object visually. This newfound inhibition reflected in infants' cautionary behavior at this age suggests the possible emergence of new control mechanisms (Schaffer and Parry, 1970).

There is some controversy as to the strength of influence that object novelty has on infants' manipulative exploration prior to 9 months of age. Rubenstein (1974), for example, allowed 6-month-olds to play with a bell for several minutes and then paired it with 10 novel objects on consecutive one-minute trials. She found that the novel objects elicited more manipulative play as well as more visual attention. However, Schaffer and his colleagues (Schaffer, Greenwood and Parry, 1972) found differential looking but no differential manipulation by infants until 8 or 9 months of age. Thus, the effect of novelty on manipulation prior to 9 months may be a fragile phenomenon, perhaps dependent on extent of familiarization or other procedural specifics.

What children do with an object, whether familiar or novel, once they have made contact with it also differs in 6- and 9-month-olds. Prior to 9 months of age, for example, infants tend to treat all similar-sized objects alike (Fenson, Kagan, Kearsley, and Zelazo, 1976). In general, objects that can be grasped will be banged on surfaces, pushed, twisted or turned, shifted from hand to hand, shaken, visually scrutinized with and without fingering and, whenever possible, brought to the mouth. Between 9 and 12 months, however, infants' manipulative behavior becomes more attuned to the specific features of an object, allowing for more efficient extraction of information about the object. For example, Ruff (1984) found that infants of 9 and 12, but not 6 months of age, are more likely to rotate objects varying in shape, more likely to finger objects differing in texture, and exhibit more shifting from hand to hand and shaking of objects which vary in weight. As several researchers have verified, there also is a corresponding decline in mouthing as the infant approaches 12 months of age.

Unlike visual exploration, object manipulation offers the possibility of various kinds of feedback. Infants also are most likely to play with objects that are reactive in some way to their manipulation. McCall (1974) found that 8- to 11-month-olds showed most interest in objects which were responsive to their actions, i.e., those with plasticity or sound potential. Variations in configural complexity alone exercised little influence on the infants' manipulative interest.

Toward the end of the first year, young children also begin to display interest in how things work, as evidenced by their growing fascination with such devices as light switches, push buttons, and hinged lids on boxes (Fenson *et al.*, 1976). This newfound mechanical interest refers not so much to cause and effect relations (such as the connection between a light switch and a lamp) but to the action of the device itself (e.g., the up and down positions of the light switch or the swinging action of a box lid). It is this latter, more focused interest in exploring mechanical devices *per se* which accounts for the allure of various types of "busy boxes" to young children around the first birthday.

Twelve to thirty-six months

There are two new developments near the beginning of the second year of life which alter infants' play in profound ways. First, infants begin to show awareness of the function or meaning of objects. That is, infants begin to accommodate their actions to culturally prescribed properties of objects. For example, American infants might push a toy car, insert a key in a lock, and throw a ball. Earlier, around 9 months of age, as Ruff (1978) has demonstrated, infants begin to adapt their actions to the perceived physical properties of objects. Their discovery and growing understanding of the functions of objects towards the end of the first year of life can now again make objects interesting, even when they are no longer novel or unfamiliar at a perceptual level.

Infants also achieve another major milestone near the one-year mark. They develop the capacity to jointly consider two or more objects and/or events (Fenson *et al.*, 1976). The importance of this new capacity can hardly be overestimated, as it sets the stage for the child's exploration of a wide range of interrelations among objects and events: *functional relations, spatial relations*, *causal relations*, and *categorical relations*. Each of these types of interrelations is readily illustrated by the play of 12- to 24-month-old children.

Attention to *functional relations*, for example, may be seen in young children's play with a tea set. They might place a cup on a saucer, a spoon in a cup, or a lid on a pot. Each of these actions not only requires knowledge of the appropriate functions of individual objects, but the ability to interrelate two objects. Young children's successful experimentation with objects of graded sizes that fit into one another (e.g., nesting cups) and their constructions with building blocks require attention to a variety of *spatial relationships* (Foreman, 1982). Understanding of spatial relationships develops in a progressive fashion. For example, children are able to duplicate a model formed by stacking one block upon another some time before they can duplicate a horizontal alignment of two adjacent blocks (Johnstone, 1981). Even duplicating the model of one block upon another, however, requires the child to consider the two blocks jointly. Children's developing appreciation of *causal relations* is often seen when they seek their mothers' assistance in various play activities. For example, in asking mother's help in removing the top to a tin containing blocks, the child shows recognition of the relation between a means (mother's help) and a goal (access to the blocks).

Finally, when young children are engaged in free play and they physically combine objects that are alike in some way, they demonstrate an ability to attend to *categorical relations* between objects. Typically, the first similarity relationships expressed by infants in free play occur at about one year of age or less and they are based on perceptual likeness (Fenson *et al.*, 1976; Starkey, 1981). In their second and third years, children show an increasing ability to match objects on the basis of functional and meaningful properties as well (Sugarman, 1981).

Like visual exploration, then, manipulative exploration reflects the steady growth of cognition. As children develop an awareness of the functional-meaningful properties of objects and gain the ability to consider relationships, they become increasingly resourceful, thoughtful, and planful. As a consequence, they progressively begin to control and regulate their play environment rather than behaving as a captive of the play setting.

As children move into the preschool years, their manipulative exploration expands into a variety of forms of sensory and motor play. These forms of play include construction activities with blocks and clay, sensory activities with water and sand, and motor activities with vehicles and climbing equipment. Each of these types of activities give young children an opportunity to explore the properties of materials, to test and develop the capabilities of their own bodies and to gain an ever-increasing degree of mastery of their world.

PRETEND PLAY

With the cognitive advances which usher in the second year of life, children spend a large amount of time in mastery play as they impose an increasing degree of order on their world by identifying, comparing, and categorizing objects and events. They enthusiastically plunge into these opportunities, accumulating a vast amount of "first-time" knowledge about the world. At the same time, they begin to show another kind of play behavior that, at first glance, might seem at odds with the goal of mastery play. They begin to pretend, sometimes simulating and sometimes distorting reality.

In the earliest form of pretence, at about one year, young children simulate some of their own daily routines, such as eating, bathing, and sleeping. Over the course of the next few years, these early pretend behaviors expand into the elaborate and whimsical make-believe play activities that seem to capture the very essence of early childhood. The first fleeting signs of whimsical pretence, however, may go entirely unnoticed, not only because they are somewhat ephemeral, but because they co-occur in time with two other major events—walking and talking. Nevertheless, the cognitive skills involved in these early pretend actions and those which follow have far-reaching implications for our understanding of both intellectual and social development. This fact, plus the especial appeal of pretend play has made this aspect of early development a popular topic of research. As a result, it is possible to describe the developmental course of pretend play in some detail.

Three trends characterize the way pretend play develops in young children. The first trend, termed *decentration* by Piaget (1962), refers to the young child's increasing tendency to incorporate other participants into pretend activities. The second trend, termed *decontextualization* by Werner and Kaplan (1963), refers to the child's increasing ability to symbolically transform objects and other aspects of the environment in the service of pretence. The third trend, which we will call *integration*, refers to the child's increasing ability to combine individual actions into coordinated behavior sequences. Each of these trends, as discussed at some length by Bretherton (1984) and by McCune-Nicolich and Fenson (1984), finds its first expression in the pretend play of children during their second year of life. We trace developments in each of these sets of skills from their onset into the preschool years.

Decentration

The child's earliest pretend acts, at about 12 months of age, are directed toward the self in the form of familiar schemes like eating and drinking from empty containers. The first decentered acts follow a few months later, taking the form of actions directed toward animate and inanimate recipients. The child, for example, might comb a doll's hair or pretend to feed a doll with an empty spoon. In these actions, the doll is treated as a passive, animate-like recipient. Even before they begin to incorporate dolls into their play schemes, children may direct these types of actions toward real persons (especially parents), as an intermediate link between themselves and animate-like objects. At about the same point in time, children also begin to incorporate inanimate objects into their pretend play. For example, a child might stir a spoon in a cup or pour pretend tea from a pot to glass.

In these early instances of decentration, the child serves as the initiator or agent. Around 24 months, however, a new class of decentered actions emerge in children's play in which "animate" participants (e.g., dolls, stuffed toys) are regarded as agents in their own right, rather than as mere passive recipients of the child's actions. Thus, a child might seat a doll in front of a table setting and place a spoon in the doll's hand rather than feed the doll directly. Or the child might in some other manner orchestrate the doll's activities, in recognition of the doll's inferred potential to act independently. (See Wolf, 1982, for an extended discussion of these aspects of pretend play.)

Children can also use language as well as gestures to attribute animacy to dolls and other objects. In fact, many children find it easier to depict internal states (wants, needs, feelings) in dolls and other "animate" objects by using words than by physically orchestrating the object's activities (Fenson, 1984). Words for internal states, in any case, appear in most children's vocabularies by 20 months of age (Bretherton and Beeghly, 1982). It is as they enter the preschool years that children begin to include themselves in their pretend dramas with others, and these scenarios eventually develop into full-fledged social roles (e.g., doctor, patient, fireman) for each participant (Miller and Garvey, 1984; Watson, 1984).

Decontextualization

The first instances of decontextualization occur when the child uses a substitute object. The earliest type of substitution occurs at about 12 months when the child uses realistic replicas (such as a doll-sized baby bottle) in an appropriate manner. The use of realistic objects is likely to be followed at about 18 months of age by the child's use of an object which resembles the intended object (Watson and Fischer, 1977). For example, the child may use a stacking ring as a donut. As the second year comes to a close and the third year of childhood unfolds, children also show further advances in their ability to transform the physical environment in the service of pretence. In the third year, for example, children become capable of using a highly nonprototypic substitute object in their pretend play. When following the lead of a model, two-year-olds may even be able to use a substitute object which has clearly defined and compelling functions of its own; for example, use of a banana as a telephone (Watson and Jackowitz, 1984). With prompting, some children of 24 months of age (Fein, 1975) or even younger are able to perform a double substitution; e.g., feeding a "horse" with a "cup", using nonprototypic substitute objects in each case. These double substitutions are not likely to occur in children's spontaneous play, however, until well into the third year or beyond.

It is in their third year that children also begin to create imaginary objects to support their play activities. Such imaginary objects may be symbolized either through gestures (e.g., petting a pretend dog), through words (e.g., "there's my little dog"), or through a combination of gestures and words. Although children under 3 years of age may be able to symbolize imaginary or absent objects via gestures or words in response to verbal requests or modeled demonstrations, this type of pretence does not become prominent in spontaneous play until well after the third birthday (Overton and Jackson, 1973). And of course, it is typically not until the fourth or fifth year that the most dramatic form of symbolic invention takes place—namely, the creation of an imaginary playmate (Manosevitz, Prentice, and Wilson, 1973).

Integration

For most of the first two years of life, exploratory play often seems to have a piecemeal quality about it as the child appears to drift from one object or activity to another. The child seems in large measure to be "controlled by" rather than "in control of" the objects or activities in the immediate environment. However, between 18 and 24 months of age, two types of linkage between successive actions appear in the child's play.

The simplest type, first seen in spontaneous play at about 18–19 months of age, involve variations on a single theme (Belsky and Most, 1981; Fenson and Ramsay, 1980); for example, a child stirs a spoon in a pot, then in a cup, or feeds two different dolls in succession. These simple pairs, termed "single scheme combinations" by Nicolich (1977), are typically followed within six months or less by the appearance of a more complex type of action sequence. This type, termed "multischeme combinations" is comprised of two or more different, interrelated schemes; for example, a child places a doll in a bed, then covers it with a blanket. The first multischemes to appear in children's play are usually limited to no more than two acts in succession. Nonetheless, they signify an important new watershed in cognitive development, paralleling in time and perhaps in importance, the transition from one to two word utterances in the child's speech. There is, in fact, some evidence that the emergence of combinatorial speech and combinatorial play reflect expression in different modes of the same underlying symbolic competencies (McCune-Nicolich, 1981; Shore, O'Connell, and Bates, 1984).

As a result of the expansion of sequential combinations in the third year, the child's play no longer so often looks like a collage of individual, unrelated actions. Rather, children are now increasingly likely to pursue mini-themes in their play, engaging in a series of interconnected actions. Recently, Fenson (1984) studied the appearance of this new continuity in play by modeling small pretend skits for children 20, 26, and 31 months of age. Three scenes (preparing breakfast, bath time, and a visit to the doctor) were modeled, in each case using a doll as the central figure. The bath time scene, for example, went as follows:

the E draws a bath by turning on imaginary water faucets over a box which serves as a tub, places a doll in the tub, adds a toy boat and an imaginary duck "for the doll to play with," rubs "soap" (a block) on a sponge and washes the doll, pours imaginary shampoo over her head, rinses the doll's hair with a cup of imaginary water from the faucet, dries her with a paper towel, combs her hair with an imaginary comb, and lets the doll look in the mirror "to see how pretty she is."

Each child's free play was observed prior to and following the modeled episodes. Fenson found that children in their third year not only incorporated more elements of the scenes into their play than did the younger children, but also exhibited longer strings of interconnected actions. The older children also showed more integration in their play prior to the modeled demonstrations. Such findings indicate that 2-year-old children are capable of a considerable degree of organization in their pretend play.

Fenson's study also examined the role of language in the children's play. Past studies of symbolic play in children under

3 years of age have focused primarily on the child's actions. Fenson independently coded action-based and language-based expressions of pretence in the three age groups. He found that, at 20 months of age, actions alone accounted for 83% of all expressions of pretence, and actions supported by language accounted for another 9% of the total. By 26 months, however, children's actions alone accounted for only 45% of all expressions of pretence, while actions supported by language accounted for 27% and language alone increased threefold, accounting for the remaining 28% of the total. As children move into the preschool period and begin to engage in full-scale dramatic play (alone and with friends), they increasingly draw upon language to identify, for themselves and for their play partners, various role assignments and imagined variations of the perceptual world. Of course, this does not mean that action fades away as a component of pretend play, but only that its role will likely change. Children use actions to implement their play dramas, but they increasingly rely on language to convey their symbolic intents.

CONCLUSION

Infants enter the world with an apparent healthy curiosity about their environment. Though they are not initially able to unilaterally alter their surroundings to a significant degree, they nonetheless learn many things about the perceptual world by simply looking at it. They begin to differentiate among objects in terms of color, size, shape, and other visually-related features. Within a matter of months, they gain the ability to use their hands, enabling them to explore a vast new array of properties of objects, including texture, weight, rigidity, and temperature. The onset of crawling and walking creates still another set of opportunities for learning. Through moving about, infants learn about distance relations and depth, about object constancy, about barriers. They experience a variety of spatial relationships: underneath, inside, outside, on top of, and behind. Through their pretend play, children are able to explore still another set of concepts, concepts centering about their role relative to other people and objects.

These various strands of exploratory play become intertwined as they emerge and remain linked as they expand into the preschool years. Though one strand may predominate in a given form of play—water play, climbing activities, easel painting, or doll play, each of these facets of exploratory play is typically present to some degree. It is largely through these playful activities that children come to define the world and their place in it.

Acknowledgement

The authors wish to thank Joseph J. Campos for his helpful comments on a prior draft of this paper.

References

Belsky, J., and Most, R.K. (1981). From exploration to play: A cross-sectional study of infant free play behavior. *Developmental psychology*, **17**, 630–639.

Berlyne, D.E. (1960). *Conflict, arousal, and curiosity*. New York: McGraw-Hill.

Bretherton, I. (1984). Representing the social world in symbolic play: Reality and fantasy. In I. Bretherton (Ed.), *Symbolic play: The development of social understanding*. New York: Academic Press.

Bretherton, I., and Beeghly, M. (1982). Talking about internal states: The acquisition of an explicit theory of mind. *Developmental psychology*, **18**, 906–921.

Caron, A.J., Caron, R.F., Caldwell, R.C. and Weiss, S.J. (1973). Infant perception of the structural properties of the face. *Developmental psychology*, **9**, 385–399.

Cohen, L.B., Gelber, E.R., and Lazar, M.A. (1971). Infant habituation to differing degrees of stimulus novelty. *Journal of experimental child psychology*, **11**, 379–389.

Fein, G.G. (1975). A transformational analysis of pretending. *Developmental psychology*, **11**, 291–296.

Fenson, L. (1984). Developmental trends for action and speech in pretend play. In I. Bretherton (Ed.), *Symbolic play: The development of social understanding*. New York: Academic Press.

Fenson, L., Kagan, J., Kearsley, R.B., and Zelazo, P.R. (1976). The developmental progression of manipulative play in the first two years. *Child development*, **47**, 232–236.

Fenson, L., and Ramsay, D.S. (1980). Decentration and integration of play in the second year of life. *Child development*, **51**, 171–178.

Fenson, L., and Ramsay, D.S. (1981). Effects of modeling action sequences on the play of twelve-, fifteen-, and nineteen-month-old children. *Child development*, **52**, 1028–1036.

Fenson, L., Sapper, V., and Minner, D.G. (1974). Attention and manipulative play in the one-year-old child. *Child development*, **45**, 757–764.

Foreman, G.E. (Ed.) (1982). *Action and thought: From sensorimotor schemes to symbolic operations*. New York: Academic Press.

Hainline, L. (1978). Developmental changes in visual scanning of face and non-face patterns by infants. *Journal of experimental child psychology*, **25**, 90–115.

Haith, M.M. (1966). The response of human newborns to visual movement. *Journal of experimental child psychology*, **3**, 235–243.

Henderson, B.B. (1984). The social context of exploratory play. In T.D. Yawkey and A.D. Pellegrini (Eds.), *Child's play: Developmental and applied*. Hillsdale, N.J.: Erlbaum.

Hutt, C. (1970). Specific and diverse exploration. In H.W. Reese and L.P. Lipsitt (Eds.), *Advances in child development and behavior*, **5**, 119–180.

Johnstone, J. (1981). On location: Thinking and talking about space. *Topics in language disorders*, **2**, 17–32.

Kagan, J. (1967). The growth of the "face" schema: Theoretical significance and methodological issues. In J. Hellmuth (Ed.), *Exceptional infant: The normal infant*, vol. 1. Seattle: Special Child Publications.

Kagan, J. (1971). *Change and continuity in infancy*. New York: Wiley.

Kagan, J., Kearsley, R.B., and Zelazo, P.R. (1978). *Infancy: Its place in human development*. Cambridge, Mass.: Harvard University Press.

Manosevitz, M., Prentice, N.M., and Wilson, F. (1973). Individual and family correlates of imaginary companions in preschool children. *Developmental psychology*, **8**, 72–79.

McCall, R.B. (1974). Exploratory manipulation and play in the human infant. *Monographs of the society for research in child development*, **39**, # 155.

McCune-Nicolich, L. (1981). Toward symbolic functioning: structure of early pretend games and potential parallels with language. *Child development*, **52**, 785–797.

McCune-Nicolich, L. and Fenson, L. (1984). Methodological issues in studying early pretend play. In T.D. Yawkey and A.D. Pellegrini (Eds.), *Child's play: Developmental and applied*. Hillsdale, N.J.: Erlbaum.

Miller, P. and Garvey, C. (1984). Mother-baby role play: Its origin in social support. In I. Bretherton (Ed.)., *Symbolic play: The development of social understanding*. New York: Academic Press.

Nicolich, L. (1977). Beyond sensorimotor intelligence: assessment of symbolic maturity through analysis of pretend play. *Merrill-Palmer quarterly*, **23**, 89–99.

Overton, W.F. and Jackson, J.P. (1973). The representation of imagined objects in action sequences: a developmental study. *Child development*, **44**, 309–314.

Papousek, H. (1967). Conditioning during early postnatal development. In Y. Brackbill and G.G. Thompson (Eds.), *Behavior in infancy and early childhood: A book of readings*. New York: Free Press.

Piaget, J. (1962). *Play, dreams, and imitation in childhood*. New York: Norton.

Rubenstein, J.L. (1974). A concordance of visual and manipulative responsiveness to novel and familiar stimuli in six-months-old infants. *Child development*, **45**, 194–195.

Rubenstein, J.L. (1976). Concordance of visual and manipulative responsiveness to novel and familiar stimuli: A function of test procedures or of prior experience? *Child Development*, **47**, 1197–1199.

Ruff, H.A. Infants' manipulative exploration of objects: Effects of age and object characteristics. *Developmental Psychology*, 1984, **20**, 9-20.

Schaffer, H.R., Greenwood, A., and Parry, M.H. (1972). The onset of wariness. *Child development*, **43**, 165–175.

Schaffer, H.R. and Parry, M.H. (1970). The effects of short-term familiarization on infants' perceptual-motor coordination in a simultaneous discrimination situation. *British journal of psychology*, **61**, 559–569.

Sherrod, L.R. (1981). Issues in cognitive-perceptual development: The special case of social stimuli. In M.E. Lamb and L.R. Sherrod (Eds.), *Infant social cognition*. Hillsdale, N.J.: Erlbaum.

Shore, C., O'Connell, B., and Bates, E. (1984). First sentences in language and symbolic play. *Developmental psychology*, **20**, 872–880.

Siqueland, E. and Delucia, C.A. (1969). Visual reinforcement of non-nutritive sucking in human infants. *Science*, **165**, 1144–1146.

Starkey, D. (1981). The origins of concept formation: Object sorting and object preference in early infancy. *Child development*, **52**, 489–497.

Sugarman, S. (1981). The cognitive basis of classification in very young children: An analysis of object-sorting trends. *Child development*, **52**, 1172–1178.

Watson, J.S. (1972). Smiling, cooing, and the game. *Merrill-Palmer quarterly*, **18**, 323–339.

Watson, M.W. (1984). Development of social role understanding. *Developmental review*, **4**, 192–213.

Watson, M.W. and Fischer, K.W. (1977). A developmental sequence of agent use in late infancy. *Child development*, **48**, 828–836.

Watson, M.W. and Jackowitz, E.R. (1984). Agents and recipient objects in the development of early symbolic play. *Child development*, **55**, 1091–1097.

Werner, H. and Kaplan, B. (1963). *Symbol formation*. New York: Wiley.

White, B. (1971). *Human infants: Experience and psychological development*. Englewood Cliffs, N.J.: Prantice-Hall.

Wohlwill, J.F. (1984). Relationships between exploration and play. In T.D. Yawkey and A.D. Pellegrini (Eds.), *Child's play: Developmental and applied*. Hillsdale, N.J.: Erlbaum.

Wolf, D. (1982). Understanding others: A longitudinal case study of the concept of independent agency. In G.E. Foreman (Ed.), *Action and thought: From sensorimotor schemes to symbolic operation*. New York: Academic Press.

Play in young children: Problems of definition, categorisation and measurement

PETER. K. SMITH, MEHRI TAKHVAR and NEIL GORE
University of Sheffield

and

RALPH VOLLSTEDT
University of Copenhagen

THE majority of play research with children has been in the preschool and infant school age range. Before the achievement of full sensorimotor intelligence during the second year, it is often difficult to distinguish play from exploration (Fenson, this volume). Later, by 7 or 8 years of age much play becomes more formalised, and we tend to talk of hobbies and games as being characteristic of middle and later childhood. Thus, preschool children of 3 to 5 years of age have been the principal subjects of investigation in areas of research such as types of play, deficits in play, play training, and the effects of toys and the physical environment on play.

In this chapter we shall examine some fundamental issues in the definition, classification and measurement of "play", especially in the preschool years. Surprisingly, many issues are not as well resolved as the volume of more applied research might suggest. The definition of play is notoriously difficult, and some investigators have virtually given up on the attempt, being content that we can often agree on whether or not a certain activity is playful, without being able to say why. Also, different types of play might need to be defined in different ways. Furthermore, how we observe play may affect the kinds of play we record. We shall start by considering what we mean by the term "play."

THE MEANING OF PLAY: PROBLEMS OF DEFINITION

One approach to this topic is to ask children what they mean by "play". King (1979) did this, in a study of four kindergarten classes in the USA. Children were observed, and later asked whether the activities they engaged in were "play" or "work". According to King, the children were fairly clear about which was which; tasks assigned by the teacher were "work", even when they were in a game format. Satisfaction, enjoyment and creativity did not distinguish between "play" and "work" activities, although King also reported that "play" activities were the ones children said they liked most. She claimed that "a lack of adult involvement seems to be a necessary ingredient of play experiences in school". However few details were presented, and it seems unlikely that children cannot conceive of adults playing with them, even if the teachers in these kindergartens did not do so in a way that the children thought of as "play".

Another study on children's conceptions of play was carried out by Chaille (1977). She interviewed 5, 7, 9 and 11 year olds about play, pretending and toys. No quantitative analyses were made of responses to the question "what is play?", but a variety of answers were obtained. Chaille reported that the idea of play as involving a lack of external constraints did increase amongst 9- and 11-year-olds, many of whom contrasted play with work.

From the work of Chaille and King, it seems that children are acquiring the use of the terms "play" and "work" from teachers' usage of the terms with them. How do adults in fact conceive of the concept "play"?

No very systematic study has been done on this topic previously, but a large number of play criteria exist and have been used or cited by researchers and educators in their attempts to define play. In a comprehensive review by Rubin, Fein and Vandenberg (1983) the following terms are claimed as distinguishing play:

1. It is intrinsically motivated.

2. It is characterised by attention to means rather than ends.

3. It is distinguished from exploratory behaviour. The latter is guided by "what is the object and what can it do?" while play is guided by "what can I do with this object?".

4. It is characterised by nonliterality or pretense.

5. It is free from externally applied rules (in contrast to games).

6. The participant is actively engaged (in contrast to day-dreaming or idling).

Rubin et al. (1983) claim that "applied additively, the features function to progressively restrict the domain of play". Thus, there is no one definition of play, as such. Rather, there are various overlapping criteria; the more of these which are present, the more certain it is that an observer will regard the behaviour as being play.

A fully explicit model along these lines was provided by Krasnor and Pepler (1980; see also Figure 1). They hypothesised that four criteria, namely flexibility, positive affect, nonliterality, and intrinsic motivation, intersect to increasingly delimit play. The first two criteria, although absent from Rubin et al.(1983), are often quoted. Their model is plausible, but no empirical support was provided. Furthermore, the use of these criteria can be questioned. King's report did not point to the importance of

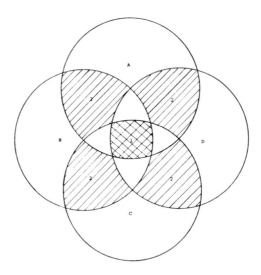

FIGURE 1   A, B, C and D represent different play criteria. If all four apply
(hatched central area) this is hypothesised to be very clearly playful. If say two
criteria apply (e.g. shaded area) then this is less playful, but still more so than if
no criteria are present. Adapted from Krasnor and Pepler (1980).

positive affect or flexibility, and Sutton-Smith and Kelly-Byrne
(1984) have argued that play need not be flexible, or voluntary.

An attempt to test the Krasnor and Pepler model was made by
Smith and Vollstedt (1985). We included the four original
criteria of Krasnor and Pepler, and a fifth, "means/ends", from
the Rubin *et al.* review. We defined them as follows:

Intrinsic motivation: The behaviour is intrinsically motivated, i.e.
it is done for its own sake and not brought about by basic bodily
needs or by external rules or social demands.

Positive affect: The behaviour shows positive affect, i.e. it is
pleasurable and enjoyable to the child.

Nonliteral: The behaviour is nonliteral, i.e. it is not carried out seriously, but has an "as if" or pretend quality.

Means/ends: The behaviour is characterised by means rather than ends, i.e. the child is more interested in the performance of the behaviour itself than in the results or outcome of the behaviour.

Flexibility: The behaviour shows flexibility, i.e. it shows some amount of variation in form or context.

To investigate the criteria, we prepared a 30 minute videotape showing a variety of preschool activities. A transcript, breaking the activities down into short action segments or episodes, was also provided. Twenty adult subjects viewed the tape and noted which episodes they thought were "play". Another ten adult subjects were used with each of the five criteria; they checked every episode to which they thought that criterion applied. These subjects were not informed that the research was about "play".

We found reasonably high consensus amongst subjects within each condition. It was highest for "play" and "nonliteral" and lowest, though still significant, for "means/ends". Thus, subjects could use the definitions reliably.

We then looked to see whether episodes characterised by one criterion were also characterised by others, and by "play" ratings. We used majority verdicts over the subjects, for these analyses. We found that "intrinsic motivation" did not correlate with any of the other criteria, or with "play". The other criteria showed reasonable agreement with each other, and with "play" ratings.

Using these four remaining criteria, we examined whether "play" was more strongly associated with the simultaneous presence of several criteria (as suggested in Figure 1). This was indeed the case. With one criterion present only, 48% of episodes were rated as "play"; this increased to 73% with two criteria present, 89% with three criteria present, and 100% with all four criteria present. The most effective criteria were "nonliteral", "positive affect" and "flexible". If at least any two of these were scored in combination, one could be 97% certain that "play" was scored; and in addition 60% of all "play" episodes were included.

These findings are supportive of Krasnor and Pepler's model, and of the validity of nonliterality, positive affect, flexibility and means rather than ends as being play criteria. It is interesting that "intrinsic motivation" was not a useful criterion. Many episodes—such as walking to another area, fastening paper, or standing and watching other children—were regarded as intrinsically motivated, but not as play. Conversely, playful episodes such as crawling or fleeing from other children were not seen as intrinsically motivated. Probably, responding to a play partner may be seen as representing external "social demands" on the child which (by our definition above) excludes intrinsic motivation.

It is interesting to note that some of the 5 year olds interviewed by Chaille (1977), actually defined play as being imposed on them. "It means if your mom says go play, you go play with your dolls or something" (5 year old). Older children replied more typically "you don't have to do work or anything, you could just go out and play around" (9 year old), or "what you do after study" (11 year old).

Perhaps, intrinsic motivation has featured so prominently in play definitions because of the strong distinction adults tend to draw in contemporary society between "play", and "work" (Sutton-Smith and Kelly-Byrne, 1984). It may be that, globally, we over-contrast the freedom of play with the sanctions of work. At a more detailed level, intrinsic motivation does not seem to distinguish play from other activities in a reliable fashion, so far as young children are concerned.

So far, we have described studies which treat "play" as a single category, or class of behaviours. But, there are clearly different types of play. For example, the "nonliterality" criterion applies to pretend play (see Christie, this volume); but most people would also describe some non-pretend activities, such as climbing and sliding, pouring sand in and out of containers, or rough-and-tumble sparring, as being play. We next consider the classification of play behaviour.

KINDS OF PLAY: PROBLEMS OF CLASSIFICATION

One of the most influential ways of classifying play comes from Piaget (1951). Piaget distinguished between practice play, symbolic play, and games with rules. These succeed each other as overlapping stages. Practice play refers to non-goal oriented actions with objects, stemming from the pleasure of the infant in having actions and objects under his or her own control—for example, banging and dropping a rattle repeatedly, or taking objects in and out of containers. Practice play emerges in the later sensorimotor period, and tends to give way later to symbolic or pretend play (see also Fenson, this volume). With the onset of the concrete operational stage at around 7 years, rule-governed games become more frequent and symbolic play less so.

Subsequent research has confirmed that functional play decreases in the preschool years, and symbolic play increases (Fein, 1981; Rubin, Watson and Jambor, 1978); though the later decrease in symbolic play predicted by Piaget for middle childhood, has not been too well documented. Critics have pointed out, correctly, that "practice play" and "symbolic play" can occur in later childhood and adulthood (e.g. Eifermann,

1971); but they are not so characteristic, with the exception of adults playing with very young children.

However it may be noted that Piaget's theorising was primarily concerned with object play, of either a social or non-social kind. Most subsequent play research has followed this orientation. Other forms of play content have been relatively neglected. For example, apart from Weir's (1962) well-cited early work, language play received little attention for many years (but see Kuczaj, this volume). Also, rough-and-tumble play was neglected until interest was revived by primate and child ethologists (Humphreys and Smith, 1984).

Probably the most used classification scheme currently, is that proposed by Smilansky (1968). Smilansky referred to the work of earlier researchers (Buhler, Isaacs, Valentine and Piaget), and then proposed a four-stage model of play development: functional play, constructive play, dramatic play, and games with rules.

Smilansky's scheme thus follows Piaget's closely (renaming practice play as functional, like Buhler, and symbolic play as dramatic), but incorporates an additional stage of constructive play. Following her own work in Israel, this scheme has also been extensively used in the USA, together with Parten's (1932) categories of social participation (unoccupied, solitary, onlooker, parallel, associative and cooperative). These two sets of categories have been used as a nested scheme recording both cognitive and social aspects of play. They have been described as "sequential, developmental hierarchies" which "have often been taken as normative" (Rubin and Krasnor, 1980), and, as such, have been used to evaluate social class differences in play behaviour (Rubin, Maioni and Hornung, 1976), and the cognitive value of preschool toys and activities (Rubin, 1977).

However, there appear to be considerable problems with some aspects of Smilansky's scheme. Her original definitions are quite lengthy descriptions, giving multiple unweighted criteria and containing value judgements. The definitions have been shortened by Rubin *et al.* (1976). They then take the form: functional—simple repetitive muscle movements with or without objects; constructive—manipulation of objects to construct or "create" something; dramatic—the substitution of an imaginary situation to satisfy the child's personal needs and wishes; games with rules—the acceptance of prearranged rules and the adjustment to these rules.

These definitions can produce high levels of inter-observer agreement and stability (e.g. Rubin, Watson and Jambor, 1978; Enslein and Fein, 1981). However, it is not clear that "constructive play" has a real place in a developmental sequence of play. If objects are "manipulated to construct or 'create' something", this suggests that the activity is accommodative rather than assimilative; some end point seems to be in view. Piaget contrasted such accommodative activities with the assimilative nature of (symbolic) play in the preschool years, postulating a tension between the two complementary processes of accommodation and assimilation which resulted in adaptation and hence cognitive growth. Thus, it would appear to be a misunderstanding of Piaget's position to postulate a stage of constructive play. Nor can precedents he found in the work of Buhler, Isaacs or Valentine. Buhler (1935) defines play as "an activity with or without materials in which bodily movement is an end in itself", and work as "the systematic effort to create a new entity". Buhler is in effect using the "means rather than ends" criterion (Rubin, Fein and Vandenberg, 1983) as the crucial distinction between play and work. Yet by this criterion, the definition of "constructive play" seems to be more similar to "work", than to "play".

The hypothesis that "constructive play" is an intermediate stage between "functional" (or practice) and "dramatic" (or symbolic) play also receives little support. Two cross-sectional studies (Rubin, Watson and Jambor, 1978; Pellegrini, 1982) found that, while functional play tended to decrease and dramatic play increase over the preschool period, there was little or no change in constructive play. The only reported longitudinal study (Rubin and Krasnor, 1980) found similar results, as does a recent study by Takhvar (in prep.).

Another report (Rubin and Maioni, 1975) found no significant correlations of constructive play with the frequency of functional or dramatic play (a finding contradictory to Smilansky's hypothesis). Dramatic play did have higher correlations than constructive play with some measures of cognitive skills. However in a further investigation Rubin (1982) found that "parallel-constructive play is highly predictive of competence", much more so than parallel-dramatic play.

The overall pattern is confused, and results are not always consistent between different studies using the same Parten and Smilansky categories. It is now well established that the Parten categories cannot be read as a straightforward developmental sequence (Smith, 1978), and this may well be true for the Smilansky categories too. It certainly seems premature to assume it has been validated as a developmental sequence or hierarchy of less and more mature forms of play.

OBSERVING PLAY: PROBLEMS OF MEASUREMENT

There are other difficulties in classifying children's play, related more to problems of measurement. These would apply to the use of the Smilansky categories, or indeed to other attempts to assess the occurrence of fantasy or dramatic play.

One problem relates to the time frame of the observations. In different studies, observers may watch a child continuously for as little as 10 seconds, or as much as 30 minutes. From the point of view of statistical independence of data, short time samples, well-separated from each other, are best. Category scores within one long sample will not be independent, thus invalidating many statistical tests. On the other hand, a longer period allows the observer much more insight into the behaviour.

This problem was brought out by Krasnor and Pepler (1980), who hypothetically argued that a behaviour (such as rolling blocks together) might first seem functional, then (as blocks are stacked up in a tower) constructive, and then (as the child pushes the blocks over and says "you're dead") as dramatic. Someone scoring the episode as a whole might rate it dramatic. Using shorter time intervals might lead to the play being scored as less "mature", or at least less often dramatic, than if longer intervals were used. In this example, it would be difficult to say which was correct; one could argue that the play did change from functional to dramatic, or that it had been dramatic all along. It does illustrate the problems of observer duration and of retrospective inference.

The problems of inference may lie much deeper than this. The definitions of "constructive play" and "dramatic play" used by Smilansky and Rubin refer to concepts in the mind of the player. How do we know if a child is intending to "create" something, or trying to satisfy his or her wishes and needs by substituting an imaginary situation? One can try to infer this from their behaviour, but another possibility is to ask them directly. In a specialised way, in clinical settings, such a procedure is used by play therapists (see Schaefer, this volume). We have tried the approach in a more general way, simply asking children "what are you doing?" after observing a play episode.

On piloting out interviews, we found that a familiar observer could get sensible replies from 3- and 4-year-olds. Some examples suggested its relevance to play classification. In one case, children were sitting on a barrel kicking their legs (functional play), but when asked what they were doing, replied that it was a galloping horse (dramatic play). Another child was washing a doll (dramatic play); when interviewed, she replied that she was just washing the doll as it was dirty (probably, constructive play).

We carried out two studies to assess more systematically whether interviews might lead to different play classifications from observation alone (Takhvar, Gore and Smith, 1984). In the first study, three experimenters were trained to over 90% agreement with the researcher on the Smilansky categories. Then, two experimenters obtained observations of functional, constructive, and dramatic play from preschool children in a nursery class. Immediately after each observation, the researcher interviewed the child, asking what he or she was doing. No leading questions were asked. The interviews were recorded by radio microphone, transcribed, and given to the third experimenter who classified them blind to the original scoring. Typical inverviews are "what's happening here?" / I'm the mummy" / "what are you doing?" / "covering the baby up" (scored as dramatic) and "what's happening here?"/"building this up"/ "what is it?"/"don't know. We're going to build it up to the ceiling", scored as constructive.

If both sets of data (observation, and interview) were comparable, something like 80% agreement might be expected, given the experimenters prior training. In fact, the overall agreement was only 34%, not significantly better than chance level. The experimenter who scored the interviews recorded many more episodes of dramatic play, than did the experimenters who made the observations.

A subsequent study was made with a much larger number of observers. Forty-six episodes of preschool children's play were edited on to a videotape, together with radio-microphone recordings of interviews with the child(ren) immediately after each episode. Another tape was prepared without the interviews. Each was divided into two halves of 23 episodes each. One group of subjects (nursery nurse trainees) saw the first 23 episodes without interviews, then the second 23 episodes with interviews. Another group of similar subjects saw the second 23 episodes without interviews, then the first 23 episodes with interviews. Each episode was scored on the Smilansky categories.

The subjects within a condition (with, or without interview) generally agreed on the classification of an episode; only 2 of the 46 episodes could not be reliably scored at all. Most episodes—32 altogether—received the same majority classification in both conditions (see Table I). However this leaves a substantial

TABLE I

Changes in classification of 46 episodes of children's play, depending on whether or not interview data is available

| | | Observation with interview | | |
		Functional	Constructive	Dramatic
Observation	Functional	4	2	6
without	Constructive	0	12	2
interview	Dramatic	2	2	16

minority of 14 episodes which received a different classification, depending on whether or not the interview data was available. The changes in classification were in various directions, but never from constructive to functional, and most commonly (8 episodes) from functional or constructive to dramatic (Table I). Here are two examples of these latter.

In one observation, the children are seen handling sticks in a non-constructive way. All the scorers rated it as functional. The interview went "what are you doing?" / "eating lollipops. And we pretend they're lollipops because they are like lollipops when you put this in, like this". Almost all the scorers who saw the filmed observation with the recorded interview, scored this as dramatic. In another observation, children seemed to be using a constructional toy to create something. The majority of scorers rated it as constructive. The interview went "what's happening here? What are you doing?"/"This is a Star Wars planet"/"A Star Wars planet? And what's that?"/"Spaceships going to the planet". The majority of scorers who heard the interview, scored this as dramatic.

This second study provided further confirmation that interview data can lead to a different classification of some episodes of play. The episode lengths here were about 30 seconds. It may be argued that a longer time for observation would remove these discrepancies. This is debatable however, as it relies on some overt sign of intention, such as a spontaneous vocalisation by the child, appearing before the activity changes. This might or might not be forthcoming.

Another objection might be that interviews are unreliable. Indeed, it may be that on occasions a child might not wish to admit certain fantasies to the observer (Davie, Hutt, Vincent and Mason, 1984). It is clearly important that the observer is familiar to the children and trusted by them. Our own impression is that the interviews generally yielded true replies. If this can be substantiated by subsequent research, then the use of interviews to supplement observations, at least when the interpretation seems at all problematical to the observer, would have much to recommend it.

CONCLUSIONS

Despite much effort, the definition of play is still in a muddle. A promising development is to consider overlapping criteria as together helping to distinguish play, rather than searching endlessly for one agreed definition. However, which criteria are useful? The concept of intrinsic motivation does not seem effective in this way. Perhaps the best we can say so far is that we probably recognise play as being enjoyable (positive affect), flexible, and most typically characterised by pretence (non-literal).

Observers of preschool children tend to rate constructive activities as play, and this too has implications for play criteria. In particular, constructive play is not obviously "dominated by means rather than ends". Why has this criterion, and that of intrinsic motivation, appeared so often in the play literature? There appears to be some disjunction between the way that "play" is commonly used, and certain preconceptions we have about play in the abstract, or ways in which we wish to think of it (cf. Sutton-Smith and Kelly-Byrne, 1984). We often take comfort from the finding that observers agree on what is play, but they may simply be reflecting a limited consensus present in our society, at one particular time.

Smilansky's scheme for categorising play has been influential, but it is doubtful, both on theoretical and empirical grounds, whether constructive play has the sequential place in it which has often been assumed. Also, the types of play recorded may be appreciably affected by the time frame of observations, and the use or not of supplementary interviews. These concerns are not just academic ones. They are all important issues if we wish to make valid judgements about the occurrence of play, and the maturity of play. Such judgements lie behind our examination of differences in play such as occur between individuals, or groups (such as handicapped/non-handicapped, or different social classes), and the extent to which play is facilitated by various child-care and educational settings.

Acknowledgements

We should like to thank the staff and children of Mushroom Lane Nursery class for their cooperation, also Andrew Mitchell, Margaret Simcox, and nursery nurse trainees at Granville College and Rother Valley College, Sheffield. Helen Cowie and Anthony Pellegrini made very helpful comments on an earlier draft. Ralph Vollstedt was in receipt of a grant from the Danish Research Council.

References

Buhler, C. (1935). *From birth to maturity*. London: Kegan Paul, Trench, Trubner & Co., Ltd.

Chaille, C. (1977). The child's conceptions of play, pretending, and toys: A developmental study of the concepts of symbolic play of 5- to 11-year old children. Unpublished Ph.D. thesis, University of California, Los Angeles.

Davie, C.E., Hutt, S.J., Vincent, E. and Mason, M. (1984). *The young child at home*. Windsor: NFER-Nelson.

Eifermann, R.R. (1971). Social play in childhood. In R.E. Herron and B. Sutton-Smith (eds.), *Child's play*. New York: Wiley.

Enslein, J.P. and Fein, G.G. (1981). Temporal and cross-situational stability of children's social and play behavior. *Developmental psychology*, **17**, 760–761.

Fein, G.G. (1981). Pretend play: An integrative review. *Child development*, 1095–1118.

Humphreys, A.P. and Smith, P.K. (1984). Rough-and-tumble in preschool and playground. In P.K. Smith (ed.), *Play in animals and humans*. Oxford: Basil Blackwell.

King, N.R. (1979). Play: The kindergartener's perspective. *The elementary school journal*, **80**, 81–87.

Krasnor, L.R. and Pepler, D.J. (1980). The study of children's play: some suggested future directions. In K.H. Rubin (ed.), *Children's play*. San Francisco: Jossey-Bass.

Parten, M.B. (1932). Social participation among preschool children. *Journal of abnormal and social psychology*, **27**, 243–269.

Pellegrini, A.D. (1982). Development of preschoolers' social-cognitive play behaviors. *Perceptual and motor skills*, **55**, 1109–1110.

Piaget, J. (1951). *Play, dreams and imitation in childhood*. London: Routledge and Kegan Paul.

Rubin, K.H. (1977).   The social and cognitive value of preschool toys and activities. *Canadian journal of behavioural science*, **9**, 382–385.

Rubin, K.H. (1982).   Nonsocial play in preschoolers: Necessarily evil? *Child development*, **53**, 651–657.

Rubin, K.H., Fein, G.G. and Vandenberg, B. (1983).   Play. In P.H. Mussen and E.M. Hetherington (eds.), *Handbook of Child Psychology* (4th ed.), vol. 4, New York: Wiley.

Rubin, K.H. and Krasnor, L.R. (1980).   Changes in the play behaviours of preschoolers: A short-term longitudinal investigation. *Canadian Journal of Behavioural Science*, **12**, 278–282.

Rubin, K.H. and Maioni, T.L. (1975).   Play preference and its relationship to egocentrism, popularity and classification skills in preschoolers. *Merrill-Palmer quarterly*, **21**, 171–179.

Rubin, K.H., Maioni, T.L. and Hornung, M. (1976).   Free play behaviors in middle- and lower-class preschoolers: Parten and Piaget revisited. *Child development*, **47**, 414–419.

Rubin, K.H., Watson, K.S. and Jambor, T.W. (1978).   Free-play behaviors in preschool and kindergarten children. *Child development*, **49**, 534–536.

Smilansky, S. (1968).   *The effects of sociodramatic play on disadvantaged preschool children*. New York: Wiley.

Smith, P.K. (1978).   A longitudinal study of social participation in preschool children: Solitary and parallel play re-examined. *Developmental psychology*, **14**, 517–523.

Smith, P.K. and Vollstedt, R. (1985). On defining play: An empirical study of the relationship between play, and various play criteria. *Child development*, **56**, 1042-1050.

Sutton-Smith, B. and Kelly-Byrne, D. (1984).   The idealization of play. In P.K. Smith (ed.), *Play in animals and humans*. Oxford: Basil Blackwell.

Takhvar, M. (in prep.).   The context of play: a longitudinal study. Ph.D. thesis, University of Sheffield, to be submitted.

Takhvar, M., Gore, N., and Smith, P.K. (1984).   The categorisation of play behaviour: Do observers underestimate fantasy play? Poster presentation to B.P.S. Developmental Section conference, Lancaster.

Weir, R. (1962).   *Language in the crib*. The Hague: Mouton.

Training of symbolic play

JAMES F. CHRISTIE

University of Kansas

ATTITUDES about the role of the teacher in children's play have undergone a dramatic change in the past several decades. Prior to the mid-1960s, most early childhood educators were schooled in the psychoanalytic theory of play. This theory held that children needed to play in order to work out their inner conflicts. The teacher's role was to set the stage for play but never to interfere with children's play activities (Spodek, 1974). It was believed that adult intervention would disrupt play and reduce its theraputic benefits.

This "hands off" attitude toward play began to change as a result of a study conducted in Israel by Sara Smilansky (1968). Smilansky had observed that low-socioeconomic status Israeli children exhibited less sociodramatic play than their middle-class counterparts. Convinced that this difference in play style had detrimental effects on the low-income children's cognitive development, Smilansky set out to teach them how to engage in sociodramatic play. The children's teachers were first shown how to use several types of play training. The teachers then intervened in the children's play and used play training to encourage them to incorporate desired behaviors, such as role playing and make-believe, into their play. Results showed that this intervention not only enhanced the quality of the children's play but also appeared to improve some aspects of their cognitive performance.

Subsequent play training studies by American, British, and Canadian researchers have supplied further evidence that adult intervention in children's play can have beneficial effects. Play training has been found to result in gains in a variety of variables, including IQ scores, creativity, perspective taking, and language development (Burns and Brainerd, 1979; Dansky, 1980; Feitelson and Ross, 1973; Rosen, 1974; Saltz, Dixon, and Johnson, 1977). Results of two recent studies indicate that the gains brought about by play training are long lasting (Christie, 1983; Smith, Dalgleish, and Herzmark, 1981). While there is some question as to why play training is effective (Smith and Syddall, 1978), the research clearly indicates that play training promotes children's cognitive growth.

Most play training procedures have focused on sociodramatic play, an advanced form of symbolic play in which groups of children plan and carry out cooperative dramatizations. Fully developed sociodramatic play contains five elements: (a) role playing, (b) make-believe transformations, (c) social interaction, (d) verbal communication, and (e) persistence (Smilansky, 1968). The following sections describe four types of play training which teachers can use to help children incorporate these elements into their play. Suggestions are then given for implementing these training procedures in the classroom.

TYPES OF PLAY TRAINING

Modeling

Modeling was one of the procedures used in the Smilansky study. Variations of this procedure were also used in many subsequent play training studies. Modeling, which Smilansky referred to as "participation in the play," requires that the teacher take on a role and actually join in the children's play. While acting out this role, the teacher demonstrates sociodramatic play behaviors that the children have not been using.

Modeling can be used to promote all five sociodramatic play elements. For example, if several children are in the housekeeping corner but are not engaging in sociodramatic play, the teacher might announce that he or she is a doctor who has come to check on the sick baby. This would demonstrate role playing and would encourage the children to adopt roles as family members. The teacher could model the use of make-believe transformations by pretending to take a doll's temperature with a pencil. Social interaction and verbal communication would be promoted by getting all of the children involved in a single dramatization. The teacher would also be demonstrating how to use verbal exchanges to assign roles, to designate the make-believe identities of objects, and to plan story lines. Persistence could be encouraged by showing the children how to extend a dramatization by adding a new element to the story line. The teacher might say, "I'm out of medicine. Why don't you go to the store and buy some more."

Smilansky and other researchers have reported that children responded very well to teacher participation in their play and readily accepted adults as play partners. Smilansky also noted that the children in her study did not become overly dependent on adult participation. In fact, as soon as the children had mastered all the elements of sociodramatic play, they preferred playing among themselves rather than with the teachers. Smilansky also reported that adult modeling did not lead to mechanical imitation on the part of the children. While the children did initially imitate the behaviors modeled by the teachers, they quickly generalized and modified these behaviors of fit their own interests and new situations.

Verbal guidance

Verbal guidance was the other type of training used by
Smilansky. When using this procedure, which Smilansky called
"outside intervention," the teacher remains outside of the play
episode and makes comments and suggestions that are designed
to encourage children to use sociodramatic play elements. These
comments are addressed to the roles that children have adopted
(or to roles that the teacher wants them to adopt) rather than to
their real identities. This is done in order to promote role playing
and to avoid disruption of the play "frame."

Verbal guidance can be used to encourage the use of all
sociodramatic play elements. If, for example, a child is engaging
in solitary functional play with a doll (i.e., simply manipulating
it) while other children are enacting a grocery store scene, the
teacher might say to the lone child, "Mrs. Phillips, your
daughter looks very hungry! Why don't you go to the store and
buy her some food." This would encourage the child to take on
the role of a parent and to use the doll as if it were a child. This
suggestion would also promote social interaction and verbal
communication by getting the child involved in the other
children's dramatization. Make-believe transformations could
be further encouraged by pointing to some unit blocks in the
store center and saying, "Be sure to buy some cereal and milk."
After the child had bought several make-believe food items at the
store, persistence could be promoted by suggesting a way to
extend the dramatization, e.g., cooking the food and serving it to
the daughter. The above examples are given to illustrate the
different elements that can be encouraged by verbal guidance. In
most instances, this much intervention is not necessary.

Verbal guidance has the advantage of being less obtrusive
than modeling. By remaining outside the play episode, the
teacher allows the children to retain more control over their
dramatizations. For this reason it is recommended that, when-

ever possible, teachers try verbal guidance first (Christie, 1982; Griffing, 1983). It this procedure fails to bring about the desired play behaviors, then modeling should be used.

Thematic-Fantasy Training

Thematic-fantasy training was developed by Eli Saltz and James Johnson for use in a series of play training studies (Saltz and Johnson, 1974; Saltz, Dixon, and Johnson, 1977). It involves helping children act out familiar fairy tales such as Three Billy Goats Gruff, Red Riding Hood, and The Three Pigs.

Any fairy tale, folk tale, or short story with a small number of characters and a simple, repetitive plot can be used as the basis for thematic-fantasy training. Saltz and Johnson applied this training in a three-step sequence that was spread over several days: 1. The teacher read the story and discussed it with the children. 2. The teacher assigned roles to the children and helped them to do a preliminary enactment of the story by serving as narrator. 3. The story was enacted several times with the children exchanging roles.

The teacher phased out his or her assistance during the dramatizations in Step 3. Saltz and Johnson found that, in order to focus the children's attention on the plot, it was best to keep the use of props and costumes to a minimum.

Thematic-fantasy training is much more structured than Smilansky's modeling and verbal guidance strategies. The children are assigned specific roles and are expected to follow a ready-made plot, whereas in Smilansky's procedures the children are encouraged to make up their own roles and to plan their own story lines. Thematic-fantasy training is therefore a simpler form of play training which focuses mainly on role-taking and make-believe. It is a good alternative form of intervention for use with children who have trouble responding to Smilansky's less structured play training procedures.

Imaginative Play Training

Imaginative play training was devised by Dorothy and Jerome Singer (1977). Variations of this procedure have been used in several studies (Freyberg, 1973; Singer and Singer, 1976; Udwin, 1983) in combination with other forms of intervention, including modeling and thematic-fantasy training.

The purpose of imaginative play training is to enhance children's make-believe skills so that they can play more imaginatively and creatively. The simplest activities focus on using parts of the body in make-believe activities, e.g., playing with finger puppets, using the hands to make shadows on the wall, and walking on a chalk line "tightrope." Next come "preplay exercises" which give children practice in using facial expressions to represent different emotions. For example, the teacher might say, "Suppose your friend breaks one of your best toys. Show me an angry face." Then activities that involve make-believe transformations are introduced. In "Blow-Me-Up," for example, one child pretends to blow up another child like a balloon. The other child then acts out what happens when a ballon deflates. Another activity, "Grey Sky," involves sitting under a large sheet of grey paper and pretending to be outside on a rainy day.

Imaginative play training is more limited in scope than other forms of play training because it focuses solely on make-believe. Little attention is given to role-playing, social interaction or any of the other sociodramatic play elements. Imaginative play training is therefore a good strategy to use with children who show little or no make-believe in their play. It can help develop these children's imaginative skills, getting them ready for the more advanced types of play training described earlier. There are also some children who engage in fully developed socio-dramatic play but who always enact very realistic stories and show little imagination in their play. More advanced types of imagination training, such as the activities developed by DeMille (1967), might help these children play more imaginatively. In one of De Mille's games, for example, the child is helped to imagine his or her mother in a series of increasingly improbable situations, culminating with the mother standing on the ceiling. Research is needed to determine if such exercises can have an impact on children's dramatic play.

USING PLAY TRAINING IN THE CLASSROOM

In order to use play training effectively, teachers should first become familiar with the different intervention strategies. The above descriptions are quite brief, and teachers may wish to consult other sources before implementing play training in their classrooms. Detailed instructions for using modeling and verbal guidance can be found in Smilansky's (1968) book and in an article by Christie (1982). McCaslin's (1980) book contains a number of folk tales and stories that can be used in thematic-fantasy training. The best source of information about imaginative play training is *Partners in Play* by Dorothy and Jerome Singer.

Second, adequate time, space, and materials should be provided for sociodramatic play. This will insure that any absence of sociodramatic play is not caused by lack of opportunity. In addition, provision of theme-related props and the proper use of space can encourage sociodramatic play (Stacker, as reported in Griffing, 1983; Walling, 1977), making direct intervention unnecessary in some instances. Articles by Griffing (1983) and Woodard (1984) contain excellent suggestions for creating a classroom environment that is conducive to sociodramatic play.

Third, the children's free play needs to be carefully observed in order to determine which children need play training.

Observation systems for this purpose can be found in Smilansky (1968) and Christie (1982). These systems are checklists which contain all the elements of sociodramatic play. The teacher watches the children during free play and checks the elements that each child exhibits. The missing elements (i.e., the ones that are not checked) then become the focus of play training.

Finally, play training can be administered on an individualized basis. The type of intervention to be used with each child will depend on several factors, including the elements that are missing in the child's play, the nature of the ongoing play situation, the child's responses to past intervention.

If observation reveals that a child exhibits none of the sociodramatic play elements, imaginative play training might be a good strategy with which to start. If the child uses make-believe but does not engage in role-playing, thematic-fantasy training would be appropriate. Smilansky's modeling and verbal guidance strategies are well suited for children who exhibit role playing and make-believe but who have difficulty interacting with other children.

The above suggestions are only general guidelines. Often the ongoing play situation will call for a different type of intervention. The child's response to past interventions also needs to be taken into consideration. If, for example, a child has not responded well to imaginative play training, then one of the other strategies should be tried.

Research has shown that play training is an effective way to promote children's cognitive performance. While play training has not been proven to be more effective than traditional types of cognitive training, it does offer one very important advantage. Play training is enjoyable for both the children and the teacher. This aura of fun and enjoyment, combined with its facilitative effects on cognitive growth, make play training an ideal teaching strategy for use with young children.

References

Burns, S.M. and Brainerd, C.J. (1979).   Effects of constructive and dramatic play on perspective taking in very young children. *Developmental psychology*, **15**, 512–521.

Christie, J.F. (1982).   Sociodramatic play training. *Young children*, **37:4**, 25–32.

Christie, J.F. (1983).   The effects of play training on young children's cognitive performance. *Journal of educational research*, **76**, 326–330.

Dansky, J.L. (1980).   Cognitive consequences of sociodramatic play and exploration training for economically disadvantaged preschoolers. *Journal of child psychology and psychiatry*, **20**, 47–58.

DeMille, R. (1973).   *Put your mother on the ceiling: Children's imagination games.* Viking, New York.

Feitelson, D. and Ross, G.S. (1973).   The neglected factor-play. *Human development*, **16**, 202–223.

Freyberg, J.T. (1973).   Increasing the imaginative play of urban disadvantaged kindergarten children through systematic training. In J.L. Singer (ed.) *The child's world of make-believe: Experimental studies of imaginative play.* Academic Press, New York.

Griffing, P. (1983).   Encouraging dramatic play in early childhood. *Young children*, **38:4**, 13–22.

McCaslin, N. (1980).   *Creative drama in the classroom*, 3rd ed. Longman, New York.

Rosen, C.E. (1974).   The effects of sociodramatic play on problem-solving behavior among culturally disadvantaged preschool children. *Child development*, **45**, 920–927.

Saltz, E., Dixon, D. and Johnson, J. (1977).   Training disadvantaged preschoolers on various fantasy activities: effects on cognitive functioning and impulse control. *Child development*, **48**, 367–380.

Saltz, E. and Johnson, J. (1974).   Training for thematic-fantasy play in culturally disadvantaged children: preliminary results. *Journal of educational psychology*, **66**, 623–630.

Singer, D.G. and Singer, J.L. (1977).   *Partners in Play: A step-by-step guide to imaginative play in children.* Harper & Row, New York.

Singer, J.L. and Singer, D.G. (1976).   Can TV stimulate imaginative play? *Journal of communication*, **26**, 74–80.

Smilansky, S. (1968).   *The effects of sociodramatic play on disadvantaged preschool children.* Wiley, New York.

Smith, P.K., Dalgleish, M. and Herzmark, G. (1981).   A comparison of the effects of fantasy play tutoring and skills tutoring in nursery classes. *International journal of behavioral development*, **4**, 421–441.

Smith, P.K. and Syddall, S. (1978).   Play and non-play tutoring in preschool children: is it play or tutoring which matters? *British journal of educational psychology*, **48**, 315–325.

Spodek, B. (1974).   The problem of play: educational or recreational? In D. Sponseller (ed.) *Play as a learning medium*. National Association for the Education of Young Children, Washington, D.C.

Udwin, O. (1983).   Imaginative play training as an intervention method with institutionalized preschool children. *British journal of educational psychology*, **53**, 32–39.

Walling, L.S. (1977).   Planning an environment: a case study. In S. Kritchevsky and E. Prescott (eds.) *Planning environments for young children: physical space*, 2nd ed. National Association for the Education of Young Children, Washington, D.C.

Woodard, C.Y. (1984).   Guidelines for facilitating sociodramatic play. *Childhood education*, **60**, 172–177.

Language play

STAN A. KUCZAJ II
Southern Methodist University

IN THIS article, I shall consider the nature of language play and the roles of such play in children's acquisition of their mother tongue.

One common type of language play is that in which children repeat all or part of a preceding model utterance. Two categories of such play can be identified: (1) imitation—those instances in which children repeat another person's preceding utterance; and (2) repetition—those instances in which children repeat their own preceding utterance. Imitation and repetition need not be immediate, although considerable disagreement exists about the maximum possible delay between the model's occurrence and the onset of the imitation or repetition (Keenan, 1977; Moerk & Moerk, 1979; Piaget, 1951, 1963; Scollon, 1976). Immediate reproductions are those in which no intervening utterances occur between the model utterance and the reproduction. Deferred imitations are those in which enough time has elapsed between the occurrence of the model and the subsequent reproduction to necessitate that some mental representation of the model has been created by the child and used as the model for the reproduction.

A second type of language play involves modifications. There are a number of types of modifications that occur in language play (Braine, 1971, 1974; Kuczaj, 1983; Snyder, 1914; Weir,

1962). Following Weir (1962), these types may be referred to as buildups, breakdowns, completions, and substitution patterns. Examples of such modifications are shown in Table I.

TABLE I
Examples of types of play modifications suggested by Weir (1962)

Type of play modification	Example
Buildup	Block yellow block look at all the yellow blocks
Breakdown	clock off clock off
Completion	and put it (pause) up there
Substitution pattern	What color blanket? What color map? What color glass?

WHAT DETERMINES THE CONTENT OF CHILDREN'S LANGUAGE PLAY?

The answer to the question of what aspects of language children play with is straightforward. Children play with all aspects of the language system—phonological, pragmatic, syntactic, and semantic. Thus, all aspects of the language system are potential materials for play.

Garvey (1977 a, b) distinguished the following types of spontaneous language play: (1) play with noises and sounds, (2) play with the linguistic system (phonological, grammatical, and semantic), (3) play with rhymes, word play, fantasy and nonsense play, and (4) play with speech acts and discourse conventions. Noise and sound play seem to be the most primitive sort of language play (Garvey, 1977a; Groos, 1901). Consistent developmental patterns are more difficult to ascertain for the remaining types of language play. Weeks (1979) summarized the current state of affairs as follows:

Perhaps all we can say for certain about the developmental order in the acquisition of language play is that children must have a minimal control over an aspect of language before they can play with it. [For example] children cannot play with words before they produce words or experiment with stress patterns in sentences before they are producing two word utterances. (Weeks, 1979, p. 112).

Thus, children seem to engage in play with different aspects of language as these aspects become meaningful to them. Given that from the earliest stages, language development involves the acquisition of phonological, syntactic, semantic, and pragmatic knowledge, children's play with each of the components from an early age should not be surprising.

SOCIAL SITUATION AND LANGUAGE PLAY

The social situation places some obvious limits on language play. Self-repetition may occur in the presence or absence of another person, but imitation necessitates another person to provide the model. Modifications may occur in either the presence or absence of another person, as may play with discourse conventions. However, language play in social situations may or may not be the same as language play in solitude. In this connection we can discriminate between three types: (1) *solitary play* is individual self-centered play which occurs in solitude; (2) *social context play* is individual self-centered play which occurs in the presence of others, none of whom is engaged in the play activity; (3) *social play* is interactive play, or that "state of engagement in which the successive, nonliteral behaviors of one partner are contingent on the nonliteral behaviors of the other partner (Garvey, 1974, p. 163)."

Just as play may be characterized as solitary, social-context, or social, children's speech may be classified according to its social function. Private speech, social-context speech, and social speech may be distinguished as follows: (1) *Private speech* is that speech which children produce when alone; (2) *Social-context speech* is that speech produced in the presence of others, but which is not produced for any communicative purpose. That is, the speech is not directed toward the present others in any sense. Like private speech, it is speech for the self and so might best be viewed as social-context monologues (Piaget, 1955); (3) *Social speech* is that speech directed toward another with some communicative intent. Such speech may or may not accurately take the other person's perspective into account, but it is nonetheless directed toward the other person.

The primary function of social speech is communication, but communication is not a function of private speech or social-context speech (although practicing of communicative skills might occur in such speech). The latter types of speech serve a multitude of functions (Fuson, 1979; Kuczaj & Bean, 1982), but I shall focus on the similarities and differences in language play in the three types of social contexts and the three types of speech contexts. The crucial variables for both the social situation of play and the social function of speech are the presence or absence of others, and their inclusion or not in the play or speech activity.

STUDIES OF SOCIAL SITUATION AND LANGUAGE PLAY

Garvey (1977a, b) suggested that play with noises and sounds and play with the linguistic system appear to be primarily nonsocial and so occur in private and social-context situations more often than in social ones. Moreover, Garvey suggested that social language play is not produced until relatively late in development. When this type of play occurs, it is most likely to be play with rhymes, word play, fantasy, and nonsense, and play with speech acts and discourse conventions. The idea, then, is that although young children may play with language in the presence of others, the play will *not* be part of the social interactions, that is, it will be nonsocial language play.

The key word in the above paragraph is *primarily*. The first types of language play are not always private (or nonsocial in social-contexts), nor are the later types always social. For example, Keenan (1974; Keenan & Klein, 1975) reported that her twin sons engaged in social sound play at the age of 1; 9 (1 year, 9 months), such play occurring in their speech when they were playing together in their bedroom in the early morning hours. In her discussion of this work, Garvey (1977a) suggested that children may need to be very well acquainted with one another in order to engage in this type of social sound play. A number of studies bear on this hypothesis, as well as the notion that social language play is a relatively late development.

Garvey (1977a, b) studied the language play of 48 dyads ranging from 2; 10 to 5; 7 for a 15-minute period. The social language play she observed increased with age, and involved spontaneous rhyming and word play, play with fantasy and nonsense, and play with speech acts and discourse conventions. However, when the children engaged in nonsocial speech (i.e., social-context monologues), they were more likely to produce noise and sound play, word play, and grammatical modifications (though they were less likely to do so than was Weir's son Anthony in his crib speech; Weir, 1962).

In another study, Heibert and Cherry (1978) studied 14 children at the age of 2; 6 in a play setting when the child was with the father, the mother, or a peer. Each child participated in each situation. The findings may be summarized as follows: (1) The children were much more likely to engage in social language play when playing with the mother or father than when playing with a peer; (2) Play with noises and sounds was by far the most frequent category of language play, perhaps because the parents provided models of such play. However, it was most frequent when the child was playing with a peer. Also, analyses of the samples revealed no sound play characterized by phonological modifications.

Rubin, Hultsch, and Peters (1971) reported that social-context speech in situations with a familiar other (e.g., a friend or parent) resulted in a higher incidence of verbal repetition and word play (about three or four times more) than was reported in other studies with unfamiliar children or adults (see Fuson, 1979, for a thorough review of the relevant literature; see also Zivin, 1979). Thus, the presence or absence of familiar others appears to be one determining factor of children's language play in private speech.

A study recently conducted in my laboratory deals with the differences that occur when children between 1; 6 and 2; 0 are placed in play situations with a totally unfamiliar peer, a peer who is a good friend, and peers who fall between these extremes. The data support Garvey's hypothesis and agree with the results of the studies cited in the preceding paragraph, in that the young children studied to date engaged in much more social language play with a good friend than with a strange peer. Moreover, language play per se (social-context and social) was less frequent the less familiar the present peer. This positive correlation between the frequency of language play and the familiarity of the present peers suggests that strange peers inhibit language play. This effect may result from a more general effect that strange peers have on young children (and adults, for that matter). Strange peers arouse scrutiny, which is incompatible with many activities, including all kinds of play, and language play in particular. However, the children that we have studied were more likely to engage in toy play than language play with strange peers, suggesting that language play is more likely to be affected by the presence of a strange peer than is play per se. Moreover, social language play appears to be more likely to be affected by the presence of a strange peer than is social-context language play, at least for young children.

The same procedure was replicated with children from 3; 6 to 4; 0. The data suggest that by this age period children have largely overcome the inhibitory effect of a strange peer. The presence of a strange peer still resulted in less social language play than did the presence of a good friend, but the difference was very slight, particularly in comparison to the difference found for the younger children. It seems, then, that young children would seem to be more susceptible to the social situation with regard to language play than are older children. In turn, this developmental pattern might reflect the older children's better mastery of the skills involved in social language play (i.e., the pragmatics that underlie successful language play.)

Along these lines, Heibert and Cherry (1978) suggested that children acquire the notion that language can be an object of play through interaction with adults. This may prove true for social language play, but seems unlikely to be true of solitary and social-context language play. The latter types of play begin at such young ages that language play with adults seems more likely to consolidate the child's propensity for play rather than to create it.

The above discussion has focused on social (or social-context) language play. Solitary or private language play has also been investigated. One of the private speech settings that has been investigated is crib speech (i.e., speech children produce while alone in their crib). Children appear to use such private speech to play with noises and sounds, all aspects of the linguistic system, fantasy and nonsense, and conversational exchanges (Jespersen, 1922; Kuczaj, 1983; Weir, 1962). However, these same sorts of play are often observed in social-context settings (Bohn, 1914; Jespersen, 1922; Johnson, 1972; Snyder, 1914).

DEVELOPMENT TRENDS IN LANGUAGE PLAY

1. Imitation/repetition

Both imitation and repetition of speech make their first appearance in early infancy (Hurlock, 1934; Johnson, 1932). Examples of such play with noises and sounds are numerous in the literature. The earliest form of vocal imitation involves sound-making during the first months of life (Piaget, 1951, 1963; Valentine, 1942). This early imitation of sound does not necessarily involve the imitation of particular sounds, but instead involves the imitation of sound per se; that is, the infant produces a sound in response to having heard a sound. Self-repetition of particular sounds appears around the age of 3 months (Britton, 1970; Lewis, 1936). The imitation of particular sounds produced by others and the ability to imitate novel sounds appear around the age of 6 months (Britton, 1970; Valentine, 1942). Valentine (1942) also reported that 9-month-olds tended to whisper when they imitated new sounds or words, suggesting to him that the children were aware of the novelty of the new forms. This hypothesis is an historical percursor of the notion that metalinguistic awareness plays a role in imitation, language play, and language development (Cazden, 1976; Clark, 1979; Kuczaj & Maratsos, 1975).

Children continue to imitate and repeat themselves as they learn words and learn to combine these words to form grammatical utterances. Children who are prone to imitate increase this activity until sometime during the second half of the second year of life, after which imitation begins to decline in frequency (Keenan, 1977; Piaget, 1962; Valentine, 1930). Similarly, self-repetition begins to decline in frequency at about 2 years. It continues to decline until approximately age 7 years, after which it remains at approximately the same level (Rubin, 1979). The decline of imitation and self-repetition most likely depends on both individual differences and the type of repetition involved (e.g., Slobin, 1968).

2. Modifications

The earliest forms of modification in language play also involve sound play (Groos, 1901; Hurlock, 1934; Leopold, 1949; Lewis, 1936). The playful manipulation of sounds, both in terms of imitation/repetition and transformation, appears quite early in development, and as such appears to be the most primitive type of verbal play (Garvey, 1977ab; Weeks, 1979). This type of play continues throughout early childhood, and from an early age involves rhythm, rhyme, and alliteration (Piaget, 1951; Stern & Stern, 1928).

As soon as children begin to combine words, the sorts of modifications described by Weir (1962) occur. Although little longitudinal evidence on this topic is available, and much of the available evidence is fragmentary, the available evidence suggests that playful modifications of syntactic and morphological constructions are most common from 1; 6 to 3; 6, after which they begin to decline. This type of play has been found in private speech (Jespersen, 1922; Weir, 1962) and in social-context speech (Britton, 1970; Johnson, 1932).

To sum up, both the frequency and the type of language play in which the child engages appear to change with age. The social situation also seems to influence both frequency and type of language play, as do individual differences and cultural factors (Weeks, 1979).

WHY DO CHILDREN PLAY WITH LANGUAGE?

Both *what* children imitate or repeat (e.g., parental expansions, Slobin, 1968; unfamiliar constituents, Ryan, 1973) and *how* children imitate or repeat models (i.e., the type of imitation or repetition) influence whether or not such processes are viewed as grammatically progressive. In addition to what and how children imitate and/or repeat, when they do so also appears to affect the developmental significance of the reproductions. Imitation during the early stages of language development seems most likely to facilitate the acquisition of words (Bloom *et al.*, 1974; Ramer, 1976; Rodgon & Kurdek, 1977; Shipley, Smith, & Gleitman, 1969), and imitation and repetition in later development are more likely to benefit syntactic and pragmatic development (Miller, 1979; Moerk, 1977; Valentine, 1942).

The developmental significance of play modifications is currently being systematically assessed with a group of 14 children (Kuczaj, 1983). Preliminary analyses suggest that the influence of play modifications on language development varies from child to child, as does the content (syntactic, pragmatic, etc.) of the play transformations. However, this variability also appears to be influenced by developmental period. Early in the acquisition process, children appear to use presleep monologues to play with and practice linguistic forms they are in the process of acquiring, although considerable individual differences are evident in the degree to which children do so. Later in the acquisition process, individual differences become even more evident; although some children seem to continue to use their presleep speech monologues to practice linguistic forms they are in the process of acquiring, other children do not practice new forms in presleep monologues but instead appear to use such monologues primarily to act out fantasies and to practice social communicative skills, carrying on imaginary conversations in their monologues.

In addition to examining the children's modifications of utterances they have just produced (which is what has been investigated in previous investigations of such play modifications), we are looking at the children's modifications of utterances others have just produced. Just as repetition has a social corollary in imitation, modifications may be either those which change one's own preceding utterance or another's preceding utterance. In repetition and in modifications of their own utterances, children produce both the antecedent and the consequent utterance. In imitation and in modification of another's utterance, the other person provides the model for the imitation and/or modification. Although our analyses are incomplete, we believe that the distinction between social language play (i.e., that in which another provides the model) and solitary language play may be an important parameter of individual differences in language play.

NEEDS AND DIRECTIONS FOR FUTURE RESEARCH

There is an obvious need for more research in this area. What is needed is a general theory of the relation of play and language development, and systematic empirical investigation of the crucial variables.

The types of language play have received differential amounts of study. Imitation has been studied in much greater detail than has repetition, and both have been studied more than the various types of play modification. In order to deepen our understanding of the influence of language play on language development, we need to understand the developmental relations of imitation, repetition, and modification. Future research should determine if imitations and repetitions are more or less common than modifications, and how the relative frequency of the types of play is affected by individual differences and/or developmental period. In addition, future research should determine if repetitions and/or modifications are subject to individual differences as are imitations.

When individual differences are found, three questions need to be considered. First, which patterns are the predominant ones? For example, are imitators or nonimitators more common? Second, how do individual differences affect language development? Third, what causes the individual differences? For instance, although some children seem to be imitators and others nonimitators, we do not know if children learn to be imitators or nonimitators or if children are somehow predisposed to become imitators or nonimitators.

Although children play with all aspects of language, longitudinal study is needed in order to determine the developmental patterns in regard to frequency of play with the various components of language. Specifying the aspects of language most likely to be played with during given developmental periods should greatly enhance our understanding of how language play is related to language development.

Finally, more work is needed to determine the relation of the social situation and language play. The social situation does appear to affect both the frequency and the type of language play. However, most of the work has demonstrated a correlation rather than causal relationships. For instance, parents who imitate their children have children who are more likely to imitate them. This does not necessarily mean that the parents' imitation causes the children's imitation. The opposite could be true. Or some other variable might affect the frequency of both parental and child imitations. Longitudinal research is sorely needed.

Note

The material presented in this article is condensed from a chapter on "language play and language acquisition" published in Volume 17 of *Advances in Child Development and Behavior* (Kuczaj, 1982). Readers who wish a more detailed treatment of the issues raised in the present article may wish to peruse the chapter on which this material is based.

References

Bloom, L., Hood, L., & Lightbown, P.M. (1974).   Imitation in language development: If, when, and why. *Cognitive psychology*, **6**, 380–420.

Bohn, W.E. (1914).   First steps in verbal expression. *Pedagogical seminary*, **21**, 578–595.

Braine, M.O. (1971).   The acquisition of language in infant and child. In C. Reed (Ed.), *The learning of language*. New York: Appleton.

Braine, M.O. (1974).   Length constraints, reduction rules, and holophrastic processes in children's word combinations. *Journal of verbal learning and verbal behavior*, **13**, 448–456.

Britton, J. (1970).   *Language and learning*. Baltimore, Maryland: Penguin.

Cazden, C.B. (1976).   Play with language and metalinguistic awareness: One dimension of language experience. In J. Bruner, J. Jolly, & K. Sylva (Eds.), *Play: Its role in development and evolution*. New York: Basic Books.

Clark, E.V. (1979).   Awareness of language: Some evidence from what children say and do. In A. Sinclair, R. Jarvella, & W. Levelt (Eds.), *The child's conception of language*. Berlin and New York: Springer-Verlag.

Fuson, K.C. (1979).   The development of self-regulating aspects of speech: A review. In G. Zivin (Ed.), *The development of self-regulation through private speech*. New York: Wiley.

Garvey, C. (1974).   Some properties of social play. *Merrill-Palmer quarterly*, **20**, 163–180.

Garvey, C. (1977a).   *Play*. Cambridge, Massachusetts: Harvard University Press.

Garvey, C. (1977b).   Play with language and speech. In S.M. Ervin-Tripp & C. Mitchell-Kernan (Eds.), *Child discourse*. New York: Academic Press.

Groos, K. (1901). *The play of man*. New York: Appleton.

Heibert, E.H., & Cherry, L.J. (1978). Language play in young children's interactions with three co-participants. In D. Farkas, W. Jacobsen, & K. Todreys (Eds.), *Papers from the fourteenth regional meeting*. Chicago. Illinois: Chicago Linguistic Society.

Hurlock, E.B. (1934). Experimental investigations of childhood play. *Psychological bulletin*, **31**, 47–66.

Jespersen, O. (1922). *Language: Its nature, development, and origin*. New York: Allen & Unwin.

Johnson, B. (1932). *Child psychology*. Baltimore, Maryland: Thomas.

Johnson, H. (1972). *Children in the nursery school*. New York: Agathon.

Keenan, E.O. (1974). Conversational competence in children. *Journal of child language*, **1**, 163–183.

Keenan, E.O. (1977). Making it last: Repetition in children's discourse. In S.M. Tripp & C. Mitchell-Kernan (Eds.), *Child discourse*. New York: Academic Press.

Keenan, E.O., & Klein, E. (1975). Coherency in children's discourse. *Journal of psycholinguistic research*, **4**, 365–380.

Kuczaj, S.A. II. (1982). Language play and language acquisition. In H. Reese (Ed.), *Advances in child development and behavior*. New York: Academic Press.

Kuczaj, S.A. II. (1983). *Crib speech and language play*. New York: Springer-Verlag.

Kuczaj, S.A. II, & Bean, A. (1982). The development of non-communicative speech systems. In S.A. Kuczaj, II (Ed.), *Language development: Language, thought, and culture*. Hillsdale, New Jersey: Erlbaum.

Kuczaj, S.A. II, & Maratsos, M.P. (1975). What children can say before they will. *Merrill-Palmer quarterly*, **21**, 89–112.

Leopold, W. (1949). *Speech development of a bilingual child*. Evanston, Illinois: Northwestern University Press.

Lewis, M.M. (1936). *Infant speech*. London: Routledge & Kegan Paul.

Miller, M. (1979). *The logic of language development in early childhood*. Berlin and New York: Springer-Verlag.

Moerk, E.L. (1977). Processes and products of imitation: Evidence that imitation is progressive. *Journal of psycholinguistic research*, **6**, 187–202.

Moerk, E.L., & Moerk, C. (1979). Quotations, imitations, and generalizations. Factual and methodological analyses. *International journal of behavioral development*, **2**, 43–72.

Piaget, J. (1951). *Play, dreams and imitation in childhood*. New York: Norton.

Piaget, J. (1955). *The language and thought of the child*. Cleveland, Ohio: Meridian.

Piaget, J. (1962).   Comments on Vygotsky's critical remarks concerning *The language and thought of the child* and *Judgment and reasoning in the child*. In L.S. Vygotsky, *Thought and language*. Cambridge, Massachusetts: M.I.T. Press.

Piaget, J. (1963).   *The origins of intelligence in children*. New York: Norton.

Ramer, A. (1976).   The function of imitation in child language. *Journal of speech and hearing research*, **19**, 700–717.

Rodgon, M.M., & Kurdek, L. (1977).   Vocal and gestural imitation in children under two years old. *Journal of genetic psychology*, **131**, 115–123.

Rubin, K.H. (1979).   The impact of the natural setting on private speech. In G. Zivin (Ed.), *The development of self-regulation through private speech*. New York: Wiley.

Rubin, K.H., Hultsch, D., & Peters, D. (1971).   Non-social speech in four-year-old children as a function of birth order and interpersonal situation. *Merrill-Palmer quarterly*, **17**, 41–50.

Ryan, J. (1973).   Interpretation and imitation in early language development. In R. Hinde & J. Stevenson-Hinde (Eds.), *Constraints on learning*. New York: Academic Press.

Scollon, R. (1976).   *Conversations with a one-year-old*. Honolulu, Hawaii: University Press of Hawaii.

Shipley, E.F., Smith, C.S., & Gleitman, L.R. (1969).   A study in the acquisition of language: Free responses to commands. *Language*, **45**, 322–342.

Slobin, D.I. (1968).   Imitation and grammatical development in children. In E. Endler, L. Boulter, & H. Osser (Eds.), *Contemporary issues in developmental psychology*. New York: Holt.

Snyder, A.D. (1914).   Notes on the talk of a two-and-a-half year old boy. *Pedagogical Seminary*, **21**, 412–424.

Stern, C., & Stern, W. (1928).   *Die kindersprache*. Leipzig.

Valentine, C. (1930).   The psychology of imitation with special reference to early childhood. *British journal of psychology*, **21**, 105–132

Valentine, C. (1942).   *The psychology of early childhood*. London: Methuen.

Weeks, T.E. (1979).   *Born to talk*. Rowley, Massachusetts: Newbury.

Weir, R. (1962). *Language in the Crib*. The Hague: Mouton.

Zivin, G. (1979).   Removing common confusions about egocentric speech, private speech and self-regulation. In G. Zivin (Ed.), *The development of self-regulation through private speech*. New York: Wiley.

Play and learning with computers

TONY SIMON

Lancashire Polytechnic

WITH THE advent of cheap microcomputer technology, many young children have found a new toy to play with. While ever growing numbers of children are encountering computers, either at early primary school, nursery school or even at home, many parents and teachers have expressed concern over two main points. These are (a) whether computers in the preschool will disrupt play and thus somehow alter the normal course of development, and (b) whether children can (or do) in fact learn anything from "playing" with computers.

One of the driving forces behind the introduction of young children to micros and of the "play ethic" of computing has been the work of Seymour Papert. Previously having worked with Piaget, Papert believes that the most valuable learning takes place when children resolve conflicts about what they do know and what they don't and so increase their understanding of the world. This mechanism was postulated by Piaget as the primary force behind cognitive development and Papert has generalised this to an opinion that such learning should be the major force in education. He asserts, therefore, that children should learn by self-directed discovery in what he calls "micro worlds". (These have been described by Yazdani (1984) as limited portions of the real world whose characteristics can easily be understood, where children build "objects to think with".) To this end, Papert and his team invented the LOGO language so that children could play with the "turtle graphics" and, as he put it, "learn maths in Mathsland" (Papert, 1980). In this way skills are supposed to be developed in the world of LOGO and then generalised into the real world to facilitate general problem-solving skills.

However, there is an opposing view of early childhood computing which does not see it as an educational panacea. This is exemplified by the fear that many teachers felt about the prospect of micros in their schools, as expressed in an impassioned article by Karen Burg (Burg, 1984). She tells how she associated the computer with Orwell's Big Brother society and with Skinnerian conditioning where, "instead of walls to hold the children inside, the computer would rely on chains of hypnotic charm". Burg is now a convert and in fact starts her paper with three examples of how a computer is help-ing individual children in a practical way in a kindergarten. Yet this illustrates a problem. The pro- and anti-computer lobbies have been polarized into opposing visions of utopian or Orwellian futures and much of this argument was fuelled by ignorance of what computers can and will do and how they can be utilised as opposed to being allowed to "take over". The blame for this can be laid at the door of academia for failing to react quickly with sufficient rigorous, objective assessment of the pros and cons of young children's interactions with computers.

Let us now examine the areas for concern, the first of which is the possible disruptive influence of computers on play. One of the most vocal examples of this fear has been a paper by Barnes & Hill (1983) subtitled "LOGO before Lego?" They stress that young children need to be active and "repetitively practice physical skills in order to gain control over their bodies and their environments" and need to experience real life situations in order to learn real life problem-solving skills. They do not believe this will happen if children spend hours and hours seated in front of a computer immersed in the artificial world of so-called "video games" or programming. Surely though this is all overemphasized. Do Barnes & Hill believe that children are going to be chained to a computer all day and never be allowed any other experiences? In fact, due to the relative expense of computers and the economic inequities in society the child/computer ratio is likely to take quite some time to uniformly drop from around one computer per 81 to 166 children, as it was in Los Angeles schools in 1983 (Brady & Hill, 1984). In these circumstances available computer time will still be minimal when compared with all other activities that children experience; thus, it can hardly be expected to disrupt normal development.

However, assuming that children will have significant exposure to a micro in the preschool where they also learn social, co-operation and perspective-taking skills, what are the main worries about disruption by the computer? Fein *et al.* (1983) outline three main areas of concern. The first is that the computer will encourage solitary activities rather than those promoting social interaction and co-operation. The second is that computer curricula will overly emphasize the preparation for school at the expense of play and creativity, and the last is that computer activities may emphasize a narrow, and perhaps inappropriate, view of young children's abilities.

Fein and her colleagues carried out a rigorous study with full experimental controls to examine the differences between activity in two nursery classrooms when computers were present and when they were not. They continued the study for four weeks since some evidence exists to suggest disruption by computer presence in the initial period (Piestrup, 1981) and this was a way in which dissipation of the effect could be measured if it occurred. The computers were introduced into the nursery as just another of the activities available and with space for children both to play with them and for other children to watch. The computers ran programs which enabled children to draw, colour and move objects around the screen by manipulating joysticks and buttons. Children could play alone or with others and often it was found that complex fantasy themes were acted out by children using objects on the screen as the focus of their stories. This suggests that the first two concerns mentioned above may not necessarily be serious worries.

The results of the study were by no means as clear cut as the prophets of either doom or boom would have us believe and in fact seemed to be mediated most strongly by factors unrelated to the computer itself. In one classroom the children became more involved with their activities when the computer was present while in the other class they became more distractable. In the first class, they were involved more in functional play when the computer was present and dramatic play levels suffered; no such changes, however, occurred in the other class. Furthermore, there was no evidence of disruption, or of dissipation of the effects that did occur, over the four week period.

In short, Fein et al. concluded that no general effects had occurred as a direct consequence of computer presence. They explain this by showing that all of the changes that occurred were mediated by the characteristics of the children and adults in the different classrooms. In answer to Barnes & Hill's point that children should not work with computers until they have reached Piaget's concrete operational stage at about seven years of age, Fein et al. conclude that "in some classrooms the computer will simply provide another route to age appropriate achievements". Surely this is a major point; so long as the computer is not disruptive to normal activity it should, if used in the right way, serve only to enrich a child's environment.

The issue of age is echoed by Krasnor & Mitterer (1983) who suggest that the optimum benefit of using a computer language like LOGO will be reaped by children at a formal operational level. This is because they should be able to use the hierarchical thinking necessary to solve the sort of problems one encounters in the LOGO "microworld". Yet there is no reason to believe that the "powerful ideas" of debugging and adaptive response to errors cannot be learned earlier since they are unlikely to depend on a foundation of formal operational thought. Indeed, as Burg encourages, once the fear has been overcome, the computer can be used to promote all kinds of learning and discovery. As she herself admits, "choosing how an educational tool will be used is the responsibility of teachers. Such choices require knowledge. Until now that's what I've lacked" (Burg, 1984). So we can see that computers are neither likely to take over the classroom and automate the children, nor are they likely to change the face of education beyond all recognition. What they might do is aid the educational process if implemented in an imaginative way. However, if teachers are to do this, they will need information about what can be learned using micros and how such ideas can be used. The hackneyed cry of "more research is needed" rings ironically true is this field; but let us examine what indications do exist at present.

Walker (1983) lists seven ways in which micros can contribute to education, among which are benefits such as more active learning, less mental drudgery, presentation via varied sensory and conceptual modes and learning being tailored more to the individual. He also lists seven reservations which include computers being hard to use, a lack of good programs and a lack of understanding about the role a computer might play in learning. A more constructive approach, however, is the one taken by Brady & Hill (1984) who ask "what are appropriate experiences on microcomputers for young children?" They then state that computers have three main roles in a class, as tools to do jobs like word-processing, as tutors where they are used to teach a child, or as tutees where the child, by programming, teaches the machine what to do.

As mentioned above, and recognised by Brady & Hill, there

has been very little true assessment of the young child/computer interaction and what has been done has often been methodologically inadequate. However, in the field of computers as tutors Paisley & Chen (1982) report that children seem to gain a sense of power when using Computer Assisted Instruction (C.A.I.) programs and that the child/computer interaction seems to be self-reinforcing. Yet Brady & Hill find that the evidence for the learning of basic maths concepts through C.A.I. is rather more equivocal. The major problem with the assessment of C.A.I. is that the results of any study will depend very greatly on the actual program that is being employed and since there is little or no standardisation, any result will really only amount to assessment of one type of experience. There has, however, been some work done on the factors that influence the amount of use of different types of software in mathematics teaching in English schools (Ridgway et al., 1984).

Perhaps more general information can be gleaned from the area of computers as tutees. Using a language like LOGO, the child chooses a goal and programs the computer to carry out the necessary steps. This is done by giving the "turtle" (either a screen cursor or a floor-crawling robot) body-centred commands like "forward", "backward", "left" or "right" and then some measure of distance. The turtle then moves accordingly and leaves a trail to show it's path. Thus a square can be drawn with four repetitions of "forward 100" (units), "right 90" (degrees). It is easy to see how this could involve a child either needing to know how to make a square before the computer can be programmed, or actually discovering certain qualities about square things in the attempt to complete the shape.

As mentioned above, this approach comes from the work of Seymour Papert. Papert's Piagetian influence led him to believe that children learn without being taught. "For example, children learn to speak...and learn enough of logic and rhetorics to get around parents—all without being taught" (Papert, 1980). The issue of how much children could learn without being taught is too complex to go into here but there is much evidence to suggest that self-discovery as a learning mechanism lacks certain important experiences which teaching can often provide.

Papert claimed that by teaching a computer to draw houses or flowers, children would automatically learn the basic rules of geometry and that this would generalise to better problem-solving skills and a whole self-discovery approach to learning. Gorman & Bourne (1983), however, found little evidence of thinking being enhanced by LOGO experience although a slight improvement in performance on rule-learning tasks was detected. Yet, as Hines (1983) found, an enormous amount of variation exists in the way that young children learn problem-solving skills through LOGO.

Such variation suggests that the claims originally made for LOGO about its beneficial effects on general thinking and problem-solving were overstated (Simon, 1984). Krasnor & Mitterer (1983) attempt to dispassionately assess the likelihood that long term exposure to the microworld learning environments of LOGO really will benefit children's general thinking abilities. They conclude that, on the basis of all that is known about the development of thinking and problem-solving, there is no reason to expect that playful learning with LOGO will facilitate improved general problem-solving skills. Yet they do believe that, for children whose logical operations are at a sufficient level to be able to appreciate the structured programming aspect of LOGO, it may prove to be a powerful tool in developing specific problem-solving skills. As for the younger child, there is some scepticism as to whether they are ready to benefit much from LOGO until around the age of six or seven (Gregg, 1978). However, when being used in a more playful way such a system may still prove very useful in allowing young children to "concretise" abstract concepts such as direction, distance and shape. This "chicken and egg" aspect of LOGO is still unanswered: whether advanced logical thought is needed in order to benefit from it, or whether it will foster the growth of such thought. This very important question is now beginning to be investigated.

The question of whether playing with computers is actually "play" is a very difficult issue to decide. The definitional characteristics of play are notoriously varied, and as Smith *et al.* (this volume) show, even one of the most widely accepted defining characteristics of play (intrinsic motivation) seems not to be used reliably by people when they try to decide whether or not a particular activity is "play". Some recent work by Fein (1985) concentrated on children's perceptions of what play and work were. A sample of 5 to 9 year olds characterised play as being voluntary, as being done "with" things (i.e. a ball), as having no external goals, rewards or externally judged performance criteria and as being done with peers. Work, however, was obligatory, meant "doing" things (like maths), had external goals, rewards and performance criteria and was done with adults.

On these criteria both Fein *et al.*'s computer play with drawing programs and Papert's vision of a LOGO learning environment fit quite well into this group of children's view of what play is. (It is interesting to note that computer arcade games seem to fail the test on at least two counts.) Only a concerted research effort that does not fall into the traps that much previous work on play and problem-solving encountered (Smith & Simon, 1984), will tell us just how valuable early childhood contact with good computer software is in terms of the development of thinking and problem-solving skills.

As we have seen, the initial shock of the microcomputer invasion seems to have abated. Alternative extremes of fear of subversion and hope of utopia have both given way to a new realism. The microcomputer is a piece of technology which is not likely to ruin children but if accepted, understood and used imaginatively, could become a tool which could enrich the educational environment of young children. It is frustrating to have to admit that we still do not know enough about just how microcomputers will be able to benefit the educational process. However, the work produced so far does give grounds for optimism and, at a time when funds for schoolbooks, more teachers and better schools are fast decreasing, any resource which governments are willing to fund (for whatever reason) should be grasped and put to its best use.

References

Barnes, B.J. and Hill, S. (1983). Should young children work with microcomputers—Logo before Lego? *The computing teacher*, May, 11–14.

Brady, E.H. and Hill, S. (1984). Young children and microcomputers. *Young children*, March, 49–61.

Burg, K. (1984). The microcomputer in the kindergarten. *Young children*, March, 28–33.

Fein, G.G. (1985). Learning in play. In J.L. Frost and S. Sunderlin (Eds.), *When Children Play*. Maryland: Association for Childhood Education International.

Fein, G.G., Campbell, P. and Schwartz, S. (1983). Microcomputers in the preschool: effects on cognitive and social behaviour. Unpublished manuscript, University of Maryland, USA.

Gorman, H. and Bourne, L. (1983). Learning to think by learning LOGO: Rule learning in third grade computer programmers. *Bulletin of the psychonomic society*, **21**, 165–167.

Gregg, L. (1978). Spatial concepts, spatial names, and the development of exocentric representations. In R. Siegler (ed.), *Children's thinking: What develops?* Hillsdale, N.J.: Erlbaum.

Hines, S. (1983). Computer programming abilities of five-year-old children. *Educational computer*, **39**, 10–12.

Krasnor, L.R. and Mitterer, J.O. (1983). LOGO and the development of general problem-solving skills. Unpublished manuscript, Brock University, Canada.

Paisley, W. and Chen, M. (1982). Children and electronic text: challenge and opportunities for the "New Literacy". Stanford University Institute for Communication Research Report.

Papert, S. (1980). *Mindstorms: Children, computers and powerful ideas.* Brighton: Harvester Press.

Piestrup, A. (1981). Field test report for Apple Educational Foundation. Unpublished manuscript.

Ridgway, J., Benzie, D., Burkhardt, H., Coupland, J., Field, G., Fraser, R. and Phillips, R. (1984). Investigating CAL? *Computers and education,* **8**, 85–92.

Simon, T. (1984). Claims for LOGO and problem-solving: who should we believe—and why? Paper presented at IT, AI and Child Development Conference, British Psychological Society, Sussex University.

Smith, P.K. and Simon, T. (1984). Object play, problem solving and creativity in children. In P.K. Smith (ed.), *Play in animals and humans.* Blackwell, Oxford.

Walker, D. (1983). Reflections on the educational potential and limitations of microcomputers. *Phi delta kappan,* **65**, 103–107.

Yazdani, M. (1984). Artificial intelligence and education: a critical overview. Research Report, University of Exeter Computer Science Department, Exeter, England.

Changing beliefs about play and handicapped children

ROY McCONKEY
St Michael's House, Dublin

How do you decide what's best for children? Although we may aspire to basing our decisions on objective evidence, too often we have to rely on our intuition, hunches or beliefs. This is certainly true when it comes to the value of play experiences in children's development. It is only during the past decade that developmental researchers began to take play seriously and started the slow process of accruing reliable and objective evidence that through time will transform some of our current beliefs to certainties and others to oblivion.

This scenario is equally applicable to decisions about the well-being of disabled people. Inevitably these are based on beliefs which in this century have veered from segregation and isolation to integration and normalisation. Moreover the topic of play in the context of disability has received scant attention. I estimate that more articles have been published in this area during the 1980's than in all previous years put together. Even then, the total comes to little over 50.

I hasten to add though, that a reliance on beliefs, convictions, intuitions—call them what you will—is not in itself a bad thing. Indeed some would argue that beliefs are a human response to an anticipated future that can but be imperfectly predicted and controlled. What is wrong is the denial that beliefs determine our behaviour or a failure to critically re-appraise our beliefs in the light of new experiences and evidence. In either instance, we run the risk of having our decisions damned as "good intentions".

Sadly the care, education and training of disabled children has had more than its fair share of well-intended decision-making. I want to pinpoint two beliefs regarding the play of handicapped children which I believe are still widespread and that conflict with available evidence. They are *"handicapped children don't play"* which is sometimes expressed as "they don't need or want to play" and secondly *"play is a good way for handicapped children to pass the time"*.

I shall end by examining what I believe to be a more tenable and productive belief, namely *"play can aid the learning of handicapped children"*.

HANDICAPPED CHILDREN DON'T PLAY

I guess this belief was widespread even among professional workers right up until the late 1960's and it still lingers on among the public. In many ways, this belief is understandable. For a start children with physical deformities of the arms and legs or those who are blind cannot play in the same way as unaffected children. Those who are profoundly handicapped and immobilised can easily give the impression of being content to lie doing nothing.

By contrast, children diagnosed as mentally handicapped or emotionally disturbed may be physically active but they behave abnormally for their age. Sometimes this can lead observers to overlook or to misinterpret genuine playful behaviours. For instance, mouthing and throwing objects are acceptable "play" actions for babies but not for 3 year olds, even if in developmental terms they are still at the baby-stage. In short, the spontaneous behaviours of disabled children fail to live up to people's expectations of what constitutes proper "play".

Another influence sustaining this belief is that those professionals charged with the care of handicapped children give priority to ensuring the children's physical well-being (the medical/nursing influence) and the development of their abilities (the educational ethos). Playfulness is hard to tolerate in the busy wards of an institution or during lessons in a classroom. Thus in the absence of opportunities for play, the belief that handicapped children didn't play became a self-fulfilling prophecy.

Although this belief may be explicable, it is certainly no longer sustainable. All the investigations reported in the literature clearly demonstrate that handicapped children do play. Unfortunately this common concensus was frequently overlooked because early studies contrasted their play with that of ordinary children and reports emphasised the differences or defects. For example, the first study by Horne and Philleo, published in 1942, involved 30 minute observations of 25, institutionalised mentally handicapped eleven year olds and an equal number of non-retarded seven year olds (equating the group roughly on mental development). The most marked difference between the two groups was in their preference for play materials; the mentally handicapped children opted for more structured equipment—pegboard and puzzles, jacks and cards whereas non-handicapped children chose more creative, open-ended activities such as building blocks, clay and drawing. These pioneering investigators also drew attention to a finding which was to recur in later studies. Frequently the researchers had to initiate the play activities with the mentally handicapped children although once begun the length of time spent on the activities was no different between the two groups.

Subsequently other investigators have described the play of groups of children who are blind (Fraiberg, 1978), deaf (Gregory, 1976), cerebral palsied (Hewett, 1970) and autistic

(Tilton and Ottinger, 1964) and while all pinpoint differences and divergencies from "normal" play behaviours, the inescapable fact is that nearly all handicapped children do play.

Two general conclusions emerge. The chronological age of the child is not a reliable guide to the type of play activities you could expect the children to show. Rather these will accord more with their "mental" or "developmental" age (Hulme and Lunzer, 1966). Secondly the children may show marked defects in particular aspects of play, whereas others may be little affected or can even excel. For example Lorna Selfe (1983) describes the remarkable drawing talent of some autistic children.

Further details of handicapped children's play is contained in the reviews of research by Mogford (1977), Quinn and Rubin (1984) and McConkey (1985).

Nonetheless, the belief that handicapped children don't play still lives on, albeit under different guises: "she's so profoundly handicapped, she can't play"; "he's more content wandering around". I admit that there are a minority of handicapped children who do not play under ordinary conditions. But just as we provide special equipment to help them walk or hear so too we need to devise extraordinary ways of encouraging their play. In recent years, two relatively straightforward ways of doing this have been discovered.

1. Soft play environments

At best these consist of a whole room filled with large, vinyl-covered foam shapes in various sizes and colours or else air-filled mattresses. Children—and adults—can romp, roll and jump in complete safety. Multiply handicapped children, those called autistic and severely mentally handicapped adults are reported to develop new play repertoires in such environments,

especially activities requiring gross-motor skills or those involving other people.

Regular swimming sessions or the use of darkened rooms with
coloured lights and soothing music are further examples of how
changes in the child's total environment can elicit play
behaviours.

2. Special toys

Children's interest in toys can be accentuated by the addition of
lights and sounds. For instance, Thomas and his colleagues
(1981) found that profoundly mentally handicapped children
could be enticed into playing with a specially-designed novel toy
which lit up and emitted sounds as the children manipulated it.
In a follow-up study, they showed that the mere addition
of lights, sounds or bright colours to a toy did not generally
attract children—so much for commonly-held beliefs! Rather
it is the effect the children produce with the toy that sustains
their play.

Recent developments in micro-electronics has led to a range of
switches that even the most physically handicapped people can
operate to activate toys, play equipment, tape recorders or
televisions; simply by blowing or sucking; breaking a light beam
or by pressing a sensitive pressure pad.

Several books are now available which give the do-it-yourself
toy-maker designs for special toys (see Appendix) and the Play
Matters organisation has an ACTIVE section which publishes
"worksheets" describing toys and equipment to aid handicapped
children's play.

In sum, the evidence and experiences already to hand
certainly convince me—and many others—that all children can
play, no matter how severe their handicap.

PLAY IS A GOOD WAY FOR HANDICAPPED CHILDREN
TO PASS THE TIME

This belief has gained credence in recent years and is well-established both among parents and professionals. To a degree it flows from changed attitudes to play in general; a tribute arguably to popular movements such as the Preschool Playgroup Associations more than the outcomes of research studies. However in the world of mental handicap services, one such study did have a marked impact. Jack Tizard (1964) removed a group of young mentally handicapped children from the wards of an institution and created, in a large house called "Brooklands", an environment which attempted to recreate the best in family and nursery practices. The spurt which occurred in the children's development, particularly in social and language skills, was substantial. Ordinary play experiences were shown to benefit handicapped children. Of course, in retrospect, such a conclusion is only remarkable against the belief that handicapped children didn't play.

If evidence from a recent survey is anything to go by, then the belief that "play is good" is certainly well established among mothers of young severely handicapped children (McEvoy and McConkey, 1983). Out of 67 questioned, all but one agreed that play is very important for children; nine out of ten felt that mothers should make time to play with their child and eight out of ten answered "I make sure my child has something to play with when I'm busy"

However for these parents—and I guess professionals likewise—there were problems. Over three-quarters felt that the child's play was repetitive; nearly half were of the opinion that their child got bored easily when they played together and eight out of ten felt that it was too dangerous to let their child play out of doors.

Experimental evidence confirms some of these reports. Riguet and Taylor (1981) contrasted the pretend play of Down's Syndrome, autistic and ordinary children (equated on developmental status) and concluded that the atypical children tended to elaborate the same idea repeatedly throughout a play period. Some twenty years earlier Hulme and Lunzer (1966) made a similar comment, "subnormal children are more content to repeat familiar routines with the different materials available, while normal children of similar mental age would be more apt to vary their use of materials" (p. 118).

In both studies, the handicapped children are chronologically older and some will have attended schools or day-centres for a number of years. It is therefore a debatable question as to how much their play behaviour has been influenced by learned routines imposed by busy teachers and care staff and how much is due to disability. If staff are to cope with large numbers of children, they are forced to resort to certain types of play activities such as table-top puzzles.

Indeed with some teachers and parents, the belief that play is a good way for children to pass the time results more from the benefits it brings to them—time to get on with other jobs—rather than to the children. These adults will probably rate as *good* play activities those which: keep the children occupied for long periods of time; do not cause too much mess which they will have to tidy up; do not result in too much noise; do not have any risk of danger to the child or other children.

Such conditions are well-nigh impossible to satisfy. All developmentally young children derive great enjoyment from switching activities, making a noise, creating a mess, taking risks and above all having an adult's attention. Not surprisingly then, some adults regress to the belief that their handicapped children do not play... at least not in the way they would like them to.

For others, the solution has been to "program" children's play in much the same way as self-help skills (feeding, dressing oneself, toileting)—using systems of rewards and prompts. A leading proponent of this approach which has emanated largely in the United States is Wehman (1977). He and his colleagues have produced more purposeful play behaviours in severely retarded adults and correspondingly reduced self-stimulating behaviours such as body-rocking and finger-flicking.

My main reservation about such methods is that any resultant gains are adult-initiated and usually adult-maintained. There is little evidence of generalisation to novel contexts—the best test of real learning. Nevertheless they can result in behaviours which everyone agrees are a better way of passing the time. It is an unresolved question whether such play is of value to the players.

PLAYS AIDS LEARNING

This belief is gaining ground so far as ordinary children are concerned but I fear that with handicapped children it is more often given lip-service than put into practice. The chief obstacle is the well-established tradition of the able-bodied doing things for handicapped people. The notion of letting handicapped children do things for themselves and in the way they want to do it, is therefore fairly radical. Nevertheless I believe we have much to learn by adopting this approach particularly in the realm of play.

An experiment with Down's Syndrome infants

Let me illustrate this with some results I and a colleague, Heather Martin, obtained in a year-long observational study involving ten Down's Syndrome infants from 52 to 104 weeks of age. They showed varying degrees of developmental delays, but at 52 weeks, their mean score on the mental scale of the Bayley Test of Infant Development was 8 months (range 4 to 9 months) and at 104 weeks it was 13 months (range 12 to 16 months).

We visited the infants at home at approximately monthly intervals to observe them and their mother playing with a ring-stacking toy. This consisted of a 1 cm dowel set in a wooden base and 13 cms high. The stack was secured to a box (12 × 10 × 6 cms) on the face of which were two small amber lights which could flash alternately in synchrony with a noise-maker (a police siren effect). The lights and sound were operated by a remote switch held by the mother and were intended to make the toy more attractive for the children. Three coloured wooden rings that could slip easily onto the stack were provided. We encouraged the mothers to play with their children but gave no further instructions as to what they should do. On most visits, the camera operator was the only other person present in the room and mothers were discouraged from interacting with her during filming.

The video-records were analysed using a corpus of defined play actions derived from past studies (see Fenson, this volume) and a sample were cross-checked by a second rater, yielding agreements of 90% for children's actions and 98% for mothers' actions.

The dominant child actions in the early part of the year were ones like mouthing, examining, hitting and dropping, although the frequency of these fell over the year. One exploratory action did increase however, that was throwing the rings.

Figure 1 charts the incidence of the six most frequently observed actions as the infants related the rings to the stack. Initially these were simple relational actions, bringing the ring into contact with the stack, e.g. by hitting it against the stack or holding it out to the face. The median age of the children when these actions were first observed was 60 weeks; range 45–80 weeks (Figure 1a)

Next the children attempted to take the ring off the stack, usually by trying to "pull it through" the stack (median age 73 weeks; range 49–87 weeks). These attempts gradually became successful (median age 77 weeks, range 50–96 weeks) although it was only from 78 weeks onwards that they resulted from

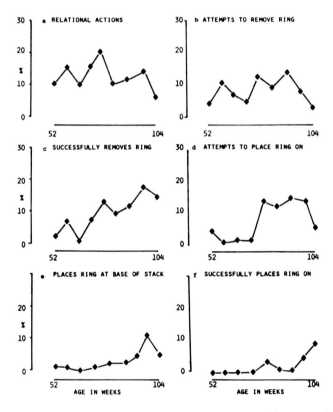

FIGURE 1   The median percentage of actions shown by the infants over the year in relating the rings to the stack.

intentional actions rather than chance, i.e. the number of attempts falls off as the successful removal of the rings increases (Figures 1b & 1c).

Attempts at placing the rings on the stack increased markedly at 78 weeks; (median age 80 weeks; range 51 to 92 weeks); the same point in time at which the infants had mastered removing the rings from the stack (Figure 1d). However these early attempts at placing rings on to the stack were often ill-defined movements with the children paying little attention to aligning the hole in the ring to the top of the stack.

Before the children mastered placing the rings on to the stack, they all did a very significant action (Figure 1e). They deliberately and carefully tried to position the ring at the base of the stack without going to the top of the stack first to get into the hole (median age 94 weeks; range 82 to 100 weeks). They knew where the ring was to end up but to get it there still needed a "detour"—a move away from the goal to the top of the stack.

Very shortly after this, as Figure 1f shows, the infants succeeded in placing the rings on to the stack (median age 98 weeks; range 85 to 104+ weeks)—although they still reverted to some of their earlier attempts at placing and rarely did they consecutively place 2 or more rings on the stack.

Figure 2 summarises the mothers' actions during the year. Invitations (hold ring out to child) and models (placing ring on stack) were the two most frequent actions and mothers' used these strategies in a complementary way.

But note the marked change in mothers' prompting when the infants were around 78 to 84 weeks of age. The reason for this may lie in the infants' behaviour at this time. As Figure 1 shows, it was around this time that the infants were successful in removing the rings from the stack and this was the time when they began to place rings on to the stack. The mothers may have felt that physical prompts were no longer required.

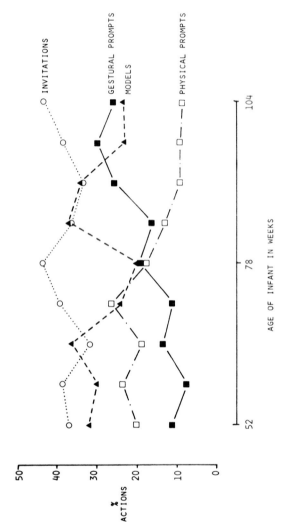

FIGURE 2   The median percentage of mothers' actions over the year when
playing with their Down's Syndrome infant and the Ring-Stacking
toy.

This data challenges some of our conceptions about teaching children to play with toys of this type. It was apparent that the mothers were focussing almost exclusively on the end-product of the task—the placing of the rings on to the stack. Their techniques of modelling and prompting were invariably directed toward this end. By contrast though, the infants perceived this task in a different way. They appeared to be striving for an understanding of the novel objects and their relationship with each other. For example, their early sensorimotor actions (e.g. mouthing and examining) could be seen as exploring the physical properties of the objects whereas the dropping and throwing actions gave the children practice in the subskill routines of grasping and releasing the rings; an essential component for successful task completion. Yet viewed from a conventional adult perspective, these actions can appear irrelevant and hence not worth encouraging.

Similarly, in the early stages, the infants had to discover how to remove the rings from the stack. The obvious way—reach, grasp and pull—did not work in this setting. Their eventual success was apparently attained through trial-and-error but it was another 20 weeks before they mastered the reverse operation—that of placing the rings on to the stack. Piaget and Inhelder (1969) have frequently noted reversibility difficulties for children when they lack adequate representations of reality.

Significantly all the children made a most insightful mistake. They carefully attempted to position the ring by the base of the stack—an action necessitating a high degree of fine-motor control. At this point we could be confident that the children's actions were being guided by some form of "mental" plan (Bruner, 1972). They were certainly not copying their mothers! Through their play the infants learnt to master the new task and moreover this learning appeared to generalise to similar tasks involved in the Bayley Test of Development such as, pegs into holes, cubes into cups, etc.

In the light of this data, it is possible to identify new ways by which adults could further the children's learning of this task right from the earliest stages. For example, the child who is just beginning to relate the rings to the stack could be encouraged to play the game of moving the rings up and down on the stack or twirling them around. If the child is attempting to remove the rings by pulling them through the stack, the rings could be placed nearer the top (adult places fist around stack with rings on top) so that the child only has to move the rings a short distance to release them. Stacks of varying lengths—short then tall—might help children master the "detour" problem. In short, the adult plays "follow-my leader"; taking his or her cue from the child's spontaneous behaviours.

GIVING PLAY A CHANCE

I have dwelt at some length on this study because it illustrates the type of research we need more of both with ordinary and handicapped children but also because it demonstrates the value of believing that play is purposeful. Nor do I mean this in the narrow sense of play as a means to an end; a central tenet in much of the play-training literature that has recently become the focus of considerable debate (Christie, this volume). Rather I would follow Vandenberg (1982), reasoning that play is valuable in and of itself. Play adds to the quality of children's life and it fosters their autonomous decision-making. No group needs these outcomes more than children born with, or who acquire, physical, mental, emotional or social disabilities. Our beliefs about what's best for them should not handicap them further.

References

Bruner, J. (1972). The nature and uses of immaturity. *American psychologist*, **27**, 1–28.

Fraiberg, S. (1978). *Insights from the blind*. Souvenir Press, London.

Gregory, H. (1976). *The deaf child and his family*. Allen and Unwin, London.

Hewett, S. (1970). *The family and the handicapped child*. Allen and Unwin, London.

Horne, B.M. and Philleo, C.C. (1942). A comparative study of the spontaneous play activities of normal and mentally defective children. *Journal of genetic psychology*, **61**, 33–46.

Hulme, I. and Lunzer, E.A. (1966). Play, language and reasoning in subnormal children. *Journal of child psychology and psychiatry*, **7**, 107–123.

McConkey, R. (1985). Play: A review of research in the field of mental handicap. In D. Lane and B. Stratford (Eds.), *Current approaches to Down's Syndrome*. Holt-Saunders: Eastbourne.

McEvoy, J. and McConkey, R. (1983). Play activities of mentally handicapped children at home and mothers' perceptions of play. *International journal of rehabilitation research*, **6**, 143–151.

Mogford, K. (1977). The play of handicapped children. In B. Tizard and D. Harvey (Eds.), *The biology of play*, Heinemann Medical Books, London.

Piaget, J. and Inhelder, B. (1969). *The psychology of the child*. Routledge and Kegan Paul, London.

Quinn, J.M. and Rubin, K.H. (1984). The play of handicapped children. In T.D. Yawkey and A.D. Pellegrini (Eds.), *Child's play: Developmental and applied*. Lawrence Erlbaum Associates, New Jersey.

Riguet, C.B. and Taylor, N.D. (1981). Symbolic play in autistic, Down's and normal children of equivalent mental age. *Journal of autism and developmental disorders*, **11**, 439–448.

Selfe, L. (1983). *Normal and anomalous drawing ability in children*. Academic Press, London.

Thomas, G.V., Phemister, M.R. and Richardson, A.M. (1981). Some conditions affecting manipulative play with objects in severely mentally handicapped children. *Child: care, health and development*, **7**, 1–20.

Tilton, J.R. and Ottinger, D.R. (1964). Comparisons of the toy play of and behaviour of autistic, retarded and normal children. *Psychological reports*, **15**, 967–975.

Tizard, J. (1964). *Community services for the mentally handicapped*. Oxford University Press, London.

Vandenberg, B. (1982). Play: A concept in need of definition? *Contributions to human development*, **6**, 15–20.

Wehman, P. (1977). *Helping the mentally retarded acquire play skills: A behavioral approach*. C.C. Thomas, Illinois.

APPENDIX

The books listed below contain many ideas about play and leisure activities specifically for children and adults who are handicapped. There are many other books on play, toys and leisure for non-handicapped children which could also prove useful.

References

Attack, S.M. (1978). *Art activities for the handicapped.* Souvenir Press, London.
Caston, D. (1983). *Easy to make toys for your handicapped child.* Souvenir Press, London.
Cotton, M. (1980). *Out of doors with handicapped people.* Souvenir Press, London.
Cotton, M. (1983). *Outdoor adventure for handicapped people.* Souvenir Press, London.
Cunningham, C. and Sloper, P. (1979). *Helping your handicapped baby.* Souvenir Press, London.
Jeffree, D.M. and Cheseldine, S. (1984). *Let's join in.* Souvenir Press, London.
Jeffree, D.M., McConkey, R. and Hewson, S. (1977). *Let me play.* Souvenir Press, London.
Lear, R. (1977). *Play helps: Toys and activities for handicapped children.* Heinemann, London.
McClintock, A. (1984). *Drama for mentally handicapped children.* Souvenir Press, London.
McConkey, R. and Jeffree, D.M. (1981). *Let's make toys.* Souvenir Press, London.
Newson, E. and Hipgrave, T. (1982). *Getting through to your handicapped child.* Cambridge University Press, London.
Newson, J. and Newson, E. (1979). *Toys and playthings in development and remediation.* Penguin, London.
Riddick, B. (1982). *Toys and play for the handicapped child.* Harmonds Worth Croom Helm, London.
Upton, G. (ed.) (1979). *Physical and creative activities for the mentally handicapped.* Cambridge University Press, London.
'Active' Worksheets and pamphlets on play ideas are obtainable from Play Matters, Toy Libraries Association, Seabrook House, Wyllyotts Manor, Darkes Lane, Potters Bar, Herts, EN6 2HL.

Play therapy

CHARLES E. SCHAEFER

The Children's Village, New York

"You can discover more about a person in an hour of play than in a year of conversation."

—Plato

THE PURPOSE of this article is to describe the three major approaches to play therapy, namely psychoanalytic, structured, and relationship. Quite diverse in nature, these theoretical approaches or schools of thought explain the therapeutic changes that occur during play in terms of different psychological processes and levels of psychic functioning.

PSYCHOANALYTIC APPROACH

In general, the psychoanalytic approach to play emphasizes the use of the therapist's interpretation of a child's words and actions, as well as the analysis of the transference relationship, to help children achieve insight into their unconscious conflicts. Melanie Klein (1937) was the first analyst to use interpretation frequently in the psychoanalysis of children and to deeply explore their unconscious. Through play activities she encouraged the child to express fantasies, anxieties, and defenses which she then interpreted. Klein felt that an analysis of the child's transference relationship with the therapist was the main way to provide insight into the child's underlying conflict. By analyzing how the child transfers to the therapist earlier experiences and feelings towards his parents, psychoanalysts attempt to understand the child's psyche and reveal this insight to the child. Thus, Klein might try to interpret a sign of negative transference by stating, "You're afraid of what I might do to you when we are alone like this?" In addition to transference, Klein would interpret the hidden meaning of a child's use of toys; for example she might suggest that by putting a doll representing a sister out of the doll house the child is expressing the desire to be alone with the parents and to be an only child again. If the father doll is then put out of the room, Klein might interpret this as meaning that the child wants the father out of the way so he can have his mother all to himself at times. Cars colliding might be interpreted as some sexual activity between child and a friend. The validity of an interpretation is inferred from the child's reaction; a telling look, a roguish smile, or a vehement denial may be taken as confirmation that the interpretation is on target.

Believing play to be the medium in which children express themselves most freely, Klein stocked the playroom with a wide variety of toys and materials designed to promote self-expression—particularly about the family situation. She advocated keeping toys simple, small, unstructured, and nonmechanical. Typically, she would offer the child freedom to select toys representing the common interests of childhood: Little wooden men and women, animals, cars, houses, balls, marbles; and other types of creative materials: Paper, scissors, plasticine, paints, and pencils. She kept each child's playthings locked in a drawer which was part of the private and intimate relationship between child and therapist. Although Klein did not allow physical attacks on herself, she did encourage the child to express deep-seated hostilities in other ways including verbal attacks on the therapist. She did not show annoyance at verbal assaults but would interpret their deeper motives so as to keep the situation under control.

In contrast to Melanie Klein, Anna Freud (1940) used interpretations much more sparingly. She employed play to a considerable extent during the early stages of treatment to get to know the child and to influence the child to like her. She would supplement play observations with information from the parents in order to gain a broad perspective on the child's problem. Only after she had gained extensive knowledge about a child would she offer direct interpretations to the child concerning the real meaning of the play behavior. Although Anna Freud later believed that a transference neurosis is possible in the treatment of children, she continued to believe that it cannot be equal to the adult variety (Freud, 1965). Moreover, Anna was careful to note that psychoanalytic treatment is not suitable for all types of children. It may be contraindicated for the psychotic and for children who have a marked difficulty in establishing a relationship due to severe emotional deprivation in early life. The presence of severe infantile neurosis and verbal facility are regarded as two prerequisites for analytic treatment. Since children are typically seen in analysis three or four times a week for an extended period, parents must have high motivation for treatment and ample financial resources. Most analysts now treat mostly latency age children (ages 7 to 11) and often supplement play with constructive projects such as playwriting, and drawings.

Anna Freud disagreed with the use of interpretations by Klein which she felt to be excessive and extreme. Klein would see symbolic meanings, especially sexual meanings, in a great many play activities. For example, Klein would state: "In his (Egon's) case, as in all analyses of boys, making a cart move along meant masturbation and coitus, making carts hit together meant coitus, and comparison of a larger cart with a smaller meant rivalry with his father or his father's penis." (Klein, 1937, p. 26). Anna Freud, on the contrary, believed that play may not necessarily be symbolic of anything. A child could enjoy making a tower just because he recently saw one.

Among the criticisms of the psychoanalytic play technique are that interpretations are difficult to make accurately and that they often impede the development of a therapeutic relationship. It has also been said that children's capacity for insight into hidden meanings is limited and that insight alone rarely leads to constructive behavior change. On the other hand, child analysts report that they have found even very young children to possess an insight ability that is greater than that of adults. Analysts also find that interpretations often help a child get in touch with feelings and motives which frequently leads to the development and anticipation of new adaptive modes of behavior. In comparison with other methods, the psychoanalytic use of play is both active in the sense of offering interpretations and nondirective in the sense of not attempting to reeducate or pressure the child towards alternate courses of action.

STRUCTURED APPROACH

Levy (1939) stimulated considerable interest in this method by reporting success with children between the ages of two and ten with "release" therapy. Rather than allowing children to play freely with a wide variety of toys and materials, Levy controlled the play by selecting a few definite toys which he felt the child needed to work out a particular problem. The probable cause of a child's difficulty was determined from the case history. For instance, if Levy noted that a specific event such as watching a monster movie seemed to precipitate night terrors he would help the child release his fears and anxieties by playing with toy monsters in the therapy sessions. The child is asked to say what the dolls are thinking and feeling during the play. This controlled situation may be repeated several times to allow release of pent-up feelings. The therapist notes or reflects the feelings that the child expresses both verbally and nonverbally in play. Moreover, the therapist plays with and sometimes for the child in order to bring out and release the assumed emotions.

Three forms of release therapy have been developed: 1. simple release of instinctual drives by encouraging the child to throw objects around the playroom, burst balloons, or suck a nursing bottle; 2. release of feelings in a standardized situation such as stimulating feelings of sibling rivalry by presenting a baby doll at a mother's breast; 3. release of feelings by recreating in play a particular stressful experience in a child's life. To illustrate the latter form of release therapy, Carl Rogers once advised his daughter to use release play therapy at home when his one-and-a-half year old granddaughter exhibited a strong fear of a specific situation (Fuch, 1957). The granddaughter became extremely frightened of bowel movements after experiencing painful eliminations in infancy due to rectal fissures. Since medical tests revealed no current organic difficulty, Rogers instructed his daughter to encourage the child to express her fears in play. The mother set aside a special time and place each day to play with the child and provided the following play objects: family dolls, brown clay, toy toilet, diaper, baby oil and cotton, and a nursing bottle. The mother refrained from initiating or directing the play in any other manner; instead she tried to reflect the child's feelings and understand the child's thoughts and motives. After a few days of play therapy the child stopped fussing about doing bowel movements and soon conquered her fear of elimination. Her mother reported that the child's anxieties about bowel movements never reappeared. This case demonstrates that the specific fears and anxieties of normal children can be treated effectively by release play therapy conducted by parents in the home.

According to the psychoanalytic theory of play (Walder, 1933), children frequently use play to repeat specific experiences which were too large or difficult to assimilate immediately. The process of repetition is an important element in release therapy because by repeatedly playing out a difficulty or loss the natural slow healing process of nature can take place. By play repetition a child can relive and gradually assimilate a stressful event and integrate it rather than denying or being overwhelmed by it. In play a child has control of the situation so that events seem less overpowering and can be mastered. Play allows a child to vicariously try out new roles or possible solutions, anticipate the future, and generally become an active problem-solver. Through play repetition a child passes from passivity to activity and thus psychically masters the impressions which were originally received in a merely passive manner. Moreover, play tends to relax a tense child and allow for substitute sources of gratification in fantasy.

Hambidge (1955) maintains that repetition is the single most important factor in structured or release therapy because only by repeated exposure to a stimulus will the child gradually show the following three signs of successful release therapy: 1. directly manipulate the dolls rather than tell them what to do; 2. become so absorbed in play that the child is oblivious of surroundings; and 3. play out primary impulses such as aggression rather than stop out of defensiveness.

Aside from the cognitive processing that occurs through repetition, it is well known that simple repetition or reexperiencing of a stressful event allows for release of tension. Over one hundred years ago Josef Breuer discovered the principle of catharsis. He observed that mental patients who were able to recall the origins of a symptom and to give uninhibited expression to the accompanying emotions were greatly improved in their overall adjustment. Expression of emotions tends to give a feeling of release from both physiological and psychological tension and this good feeling gives one courage to attack problems so that creative energy is activated. Playing out or talking out intense emotions also lessens the likelihood one will act out hurt feelings. This emotional purging has come to be recognized as one aspect of a more general process in which the patient—with the accepting, encouraging, and supportive friendship of the therapist—is helped to give full expression to previously bottled-up conflicts, fears, and anxieties. This general process is called ventilation and it seems to account for a significant portion of the total therapeutic impact of all psychotherapies (Schofield, 1964). It is well known that simple repetition or reexperiencing of a stressful event allows for release of tension.

In summary, structuring a child's play so he or she reexperiences a stressful situation can not only allow for a release of pent-up emotions but also assist the child to cognitively assimilate the event and master it. In general it takes frequent repetition of the stimulus for this "working through" process to occur. The encouragement of a supportive therapist or parent is needed to get the child to keep facing strong hurtful emotions and gradually overcome them.

A pitfall to avoid in release therapy is to come on too strong so that emotional "flooding" occurs, that is, a release of a massive amount of negative feelings so that the child is overwhelmed and regresses or disintegrates. Structured or release therapy should only be employed when a positive therapeutic relationship is firmly established and the child is judged to possess sufficient ego strength to tolerate an emotional upheaval. It should be recognized that the feelings of troubled children are quite deep and powerful. It has been found, for instance, that emotionally disturbed children differ from normal children not in the content of their play (normal children reveal just as many bloodthirsty killings and mutilations) but in the intensity of feelings. Moustakas (1955) observed that normal four year olds expressed more open and direct hostility to their siblings than the disturbed group, but the intensity ratings for such expressions were significantly higher for the latter.

A major advantage of structured play therapy is that it increases the specificity of treatment. It can save hours of time by not indulging in periods of diffuse, haphazard, and uneventful therapy. As a result, the most recent trend in play therapy is toward the use of structured techniques to encourage a child to express emotions without undue delay. Among the more recent techniques for structuring play therapy are the mutual story-telling technique (Gardner 1971), and dramatic or role playing techniques such as costume play therapy (Marcus 1966) and hand puppets (Woltmann, 1972). Most play therapists now incorporate a mixture of free and structured play in their work with children.

RELATIONSHIP APPROACH

Rooted in the writings of Otto Rank, Frederick Allen and Carl Rogers, nondirective therapy emphasizes the importance of the relationship between therapist and child. The therapist endeavors to create a playroom atmosphere in which the child feels fully accepted, respected, and understood. In this way it is felt that the child is free to experience and realize his own inner world and activate his self-curative powers and innate potential for growth. Self-awareness and self-direction by the child are the goals of this approach. The therapist operates by avoiding criticism, advice, interpretations and directions; rather the child is provided with a well-stocked playroom and given the freedom to play as he wishes or remain silent. The therapist is not a passive onlooker but actively observes and reflects the child's thoughts and feelings and tries to empathically understand the world from the child's perspective. Thus, empathy, genuineness, encouragement and listening skills are the key aspects of this new child-adult relationship.

A basic premise of nondirective therapy is that when a child's feelings are expressed, identified, and accepted, the child can accept them more and is better able to integrate and deal with them. The therapist helps by not only providing toys and materials that elicit self-expressions, but by reflecting or being a mirror to the feelings of the child and accepting these negative feelings so the child can also accept them without thinking himself abnormal or "bad" because he has them.

The therapeutic process in play seems to pass through four distinct phases. At first the child exhibits diffuse, undifferentiated emotions that are very negative in nature. Thus, disturbed children either want to destroy everything or to be left alone in silence. As the therapeutic relationship grows the children are able to express anger more specifically such as towards a parent or sibling. When these negative feelings are accepted the child begins to accept himself more and feel worthwhile. This leads to the third stage wherein the child is able to express positive feelings. He shows considerable ambivalence in this stage so that his kindly feelings are interspersed with hostile ones. He will hug a doll one moment and yell at it or attempt to hurt it the next. The ambivalent feelings tend to be intense and irrational in the beginning but as the positive emotions become stronger the child enters the final stage in which he is able to separate and express more realistically his positive and negative emotions.

According to Axline (1969), the eight basic principles which guide the non-directive therapist are simple:

1. The therapist must develop a warm, friendly relationship with the child as quickly as possible.

2. The therapist must accept the child exactly as is.

3. The therapist must be permissive and allow the children freedom to express feelings completely.

4. The therapist reflects back the child's *feelings* to help child gain insight into own behavior.

5. The therapist shows a deep respect for child's ability to solve own problems when given the opportunity. Responsibility for decision making and change is left with the child.

6. The therapist does not attempt to direct a child's behavior or conversation in any way. The child takes the initiative and the therapist follows. The child is in charge in the playroom.

7. The therapist does not attempt to hurry the therapy which is seen as a gradual process.

8. The therapist only sets those limits necessary to make the child responsible for the relationship.

Moustakas (1966) has stressed the importance of genuineness or authenticity in the therapist-child relationship. In the existential tradition he highlights the need to tune in to concretely felt here-and-now experiences in the relationship. For example, the therapist should try to own and express personal reactions; the therapist might say, "I'm happy about that. How do you feel about it?" In this way the child is helped to differentiate his own feelings, find meaning in his life, and to discover his unique selfhood. Loss of self, according to Moustakas, is the central problem of the disturbed child. Moustakas currently calls his form of relationship therapy "experiential or existential child therapy." Rather than playing a role, the therapist communicates his or her real self to the child.

Relationship therapy is based upon a particular theory of personality which assumes that an individual has within himself, not only the ability to solve his own problems, but also a growth force that makes mature behavior more satisfying than immature behavior. Once a child experiences a relationship in which he feels accepted, respected, and understood, his creative forces are released which drive him towards a full, healthy, self-directed life. According to Axline (1969, p. 74), "The relationship that is created between the therapist and the child is the deciding factor in the success or failure of the therapy." Research has supported this position that the most important aspect of effective psychotherapy is the interpersonal skills of the therapist, the relationship itself rather than techniques. The critical interpersonal skills of the therapist seem to be empathy or the ability to "be with" the child, nonpossessive warmth, and genuineness or coming across as a real person (Truax & Carkhuff, 1967).

Because of the apparent simplicity of the concepts and the popularity of the writing of Axline and others, nondirective counseling has come to be regarded as *the* approach to play therapy. This is unfortunate because it tends to encourage the forcing of children into a rigid mold rather than flexibly selecting methods to fit the needs of the child. There are signs, however, that many therapists are now attempting to accelerate the nondirective therapy process by introducing structured techniques at selected intervals. Another trend in nondirective play therapy is to train paraprofessionals, such as parents (Stover & Guerney, 1967) and college students (Linden & Stollak, 1969), to be play therapists. Preliminary studies by Guerney and Stollak indicate that it is possible to train a wide variety of people to use nondirective methods with children.

CONCLUSION

Common to all the major approaches to play therapy is the belief that play has a powerful therapeutic value for a child with emotional and/or behavior problems. According to Piaget

(1969), active experimentation and repetition in play enables children to "mentally digest" and assimilate novel situations and experiences. White (1966) stressed that problem-solving and competence skills develop through play activities. Children deal with daily experiences by creating similar situations in play and then mastering these events by experiment and planning. In play the child is in control of the happenings and there is less anxiety because it is a low-risk situation. Erikson (1963) stated that play is a kind of "emotional laboratory" in which the child learns to master his environment and come to terms with the world. He said that to "play-it-out" is the most natural and self-healing process in childhood.

Among the curative powers of play are the following: It releases tensions and pent-up emotions; it allows for compensation in fantasy for loss, hurts, and failures; it facilitates self-discovery of more adaptive behaviors; it promotes awareness of conflicts revealed only symbolically or through displacement; and it offers the opportunity to reeducate children to alternate behaviors through role playing or story telling. The therapeutic usefulness of play is also based on the fact that play is the child's natural mode of self-expression, just as talk is the natural form of communication for the adult. Ginott (1961) noted that "the child's play is his talk and toys are his words." Play also represents a way of establishing rapport and friendly contact with a child since it is an activity that is interesting, enjoyable, and natural to children.

In summary, Nickerson (1973) listed the following reasons why play activities remain the main therapeutic approach for both individual and group work with children:

1. Play is a child's natural medium for self-expression, experimentation and learning.

2. Feeling at home in a play setting, the child can readily relate to toys and play out concerns with them.

3. A play medium facilitates a child's communication and expression.

4. A play medium also allows for a cathartic release of feelings, frustrations, and so on.

5. Play experience can be renewing, wholesome and constructive in a child's life.

6. The adult can more naturally understand the child's world by observing him or her at play, and can more readily relate to the child via play activities than through an entirely verbal discussion.

References

Axline, V. (1969). *Play therapy.* Ballantine, New York.

Erikson, E.H. (1963). Toys and Reason (Chapter 6) in *Childhood and society.* W.W. Norton and Co., New York.

Freud, A. (1940). *The psycho-analytical treatment of children.* Imago, London.

Freud, A. (1965). *Normality and pathology in childhood.* International Universities Press, New York.

Fuch, N.R. (1957). Play therapy at home. *Merrill-Palmer quarterly,* **3**, 89–95.

Gardner, R.A. (1971). *Therapeutic communication with children: The mutual storytelling technique.* Science House, New York.

Ginott, H.G. (1961). *Group psychotherapy with children.* McGraw-Hill, New York.

Hambidge, G. (1955). Structured play therapy. *American journal of orthopsychiatry,* **25**, 601–617.

Klein, M. (1937). *The psychoanalysis of children.* 2nd. Ed. Hogarth Press, London.

Levy, D.M. (1939). Release therapy. *American journal of orthopsychiatry,* **9**, 713–736.

Linden, J.I. and Stollak, G.E. (1969). The training of undergraduates in play technique. *Journal of clinical psychology,* **25**, 213–218.

Marcus, I.D. (1966). Costume play therapy. *American academy of child psychiatry journal,* **5**, 441–451.

Moustakas, E.E. (1955). The frequency and intensity of negative attitude expressed in play therapy: a comparison of well-adjusted and disturbed children. *Journal of genetic psychology,* **86**, 309–325.

Moustakas, C. (1966). *The child's discovery of himself.* Ballantine, New York.

Nickerson, E.T. (1973).   Psychology of play and play therapy in classroom activities. *Educating children*, Spring; 1–6.

Piaget, J. (1969).   *The mechanisms of perception.* Basic Books, New York.

Stover, L. and Guerney, B.G. (1967).   The efficacy of training procedures for mothers in filial therapy. *Psychotherapy: theory, research and practice,* **4**, 110–115.

Truax, C.B. and Carkhuff, R.R. (1967).   *Toward effective counseling and psychotherapy.* Aldine, Chicago.

Walder, R. (1933).   The psychoanalytic theory of play. *Psychoanalytic quarterly,* **2**, 208–224.

White, R.W. (1966).   *Lives in progress.* 2nd Ed. Holt, Rinehart, and Winston, New York.

Woltmann, A.G. (1972).   Puppetry as a tool in child psychotherapy. *International journal of child psychiatry,* **1**, 84–96.

Outdoor play and play equipment

HEATHER NAYLOR
University of Surrey

PLAY does not occur "in a vacuum", rather it happens *within a context*. This context will have physical and social dimensions. Without an understanding of what that context is and of how it affects a child's play, we cannot hope to gain a full understanding of the phenomenon. Children play with something and/or someone (even if only in imagination), in a certain place and at a certain time. These other factors may not have as much effect on the child's play as will the child's own propensities of the moment; nevertheless they will have some effect and as such should not be ignored.

Play arises through the interaction of factors within the individual with those resident in the environment. Player factors will be both genetically and experientially determined and may refer to motivational states as adjusted by previous experience. Environmental factors will include both the physical characteristics of play things and those of the surroundings, physical laws, and the current social environment and its "laws". An interactive model of player and environment has been drawn up by Gehlbach (1980), who conceptualises play as a behavioural system, all components of which must be simultaneously represented if any one of them is to be understood properly.

I shall consider here some aspects of the play environment, and its effect on children's play behaviour.

INDOOR OR OUTDOOR ENVIRONMENTS?

All possible places to play can be described as either indoor or
outdoors. It seems clear that the two domains differ spatially,
socially and with respect to the activities that happen there.
Moore and Young (1978) assert that: "For children 'indoors' is
a private domain, the source of physical shelter, social security
and psychic support—and also the locus of adult dominance and
the limiting effects of 'family' and 'school'. 'Outdoors' is a
necessary counterbalance, an explorable public domain providing engagement with living systems and the prevailing culture—
the locus of volitional learning."

Essentially "outdoors" is in all ways larger than "indoors",
providing a setting for games and play involving more people,
bigger movements, balls and so forth. It has a variety of terrains:
smooth surfaces for wheels, grass for soft landings, soil for
digging and vegetation for hiding in. It permits varied social
interaction as other children and adults pass through it. It is
non-static, being subject both to changes in weather and to
seasonal changes in flora and fauna. It can therefore be a
continual source of novelty for a child.

Some authors assert that it is vital for children to have contact
with outdoor or natural environments. Shafer (1977) maintains
that without an awareness and appreciation of the dependence
of life on natural environments gained as children, adults will
not make intelligent decisions about the use, management and
protection of such basic life support systems as air, water, soil
and flora and fauna. The importance of contact with nature for
psychological well-being is emphasised by Kaplan (1977). He
says that "For some, nature is a source of tranquility". The
"absence of confusion" associated with a nature experience can
be, says Kaplan, highly pleasurable, and if occuring "at a time
when issues of identity and one's relationship to the environment

are pressing, could have a lasting impact on the character and functioning of the individual." (Kaplan 1977).

Whilst these tenets could never be proven, the ideas are interesting and intuitively appealing. Contact with nature could be defended on the grounds that it allows learning of new concepts in a new and changing environment, investigation of the ecology of the natural world, experimentation with natural materials etc., without recourse to more sophisticated psychological ideas.

Despite the apparent attractiveness of outdoor environments for play, children's actual use of them rather than indoor places does not entirely bear this out. Barker and Wright (1955) in their study of an American town, state that 43% of children's waking hours were spent in community (i.e. non-indoors) settings, of which only a proportion would be play settings. A Department of the Environment report (1973) provides data on the spatial behaviour of children on a London housing estate: the overall aggregate proportion of all resident children seen outdoors during the day was only 22%; for 5–10 year olds it was 30%. However when interviewed concerning what they liked about where they lived, 75% of the 237 children answered in terms of "places to play outdoors" (p. 76).

This contrast between actual use of the outdoors for play and professed liking for it could be explained by a number of reasons. Firstly, inconsistency within the children between their thoughts and actions. Secondly, constraints on the children prohibiting them carrying out their desired actions. As well as parental constraints, the child's own competence level will set limits on behaviour, and such mundane things as the weather will also limit time spent outdoors. So far, most research effort has been directed towards the latter explanations, rather than investigating the congruence between thought and action in children.

FACTORS AFFECTING THE USE OF OUTDOOR ENVIRONMENTS FOR PLAY

It is impossible to entirely separate physical factors determining play from those residing in the child, as it is the interaction between the child and environment that is vital to the production of the final play activity. However, for ease of comprehension the factors have been grouped here under two headings as appropriate although this classification is by no means definitive.

Environmental factors

1. Weather and time   There are strong seasonal variations in the use of outdoor places for play, with peaks in the summer and the lowest use in the winter. This is partly attributable to the improved temperature and weather conditions of the summer and partly to the longer hours of daylight. These trends are well documented by Moore (1974) in his all-year round study of a playground. Countries with different weather conditions will have different levels of outdoor play. Baker (1977) contrasts how a child in Britain has often to remain in the house because of adverse weather conditions, whereas in many tropical areas the outdoor environment is available all year round.

As well as daylight constraints upon time outdoors, so the everyday pattern of living will determine when children may play outdoors. Surveys of playground use (Moore 1974, Allen 1968, Hole 1966) have shown that small children below school age use them during the mornings and afternoons with a lull at lunchtime. After 4 pm it is mostly school age children and teenagers. At weekends and during school holidays children of all ages use them. It is to be expected that this patterning of use will apply to other places but so far this has not been systematically studied.

2. *Local landscape*   If home for a child is in a residential area, then a different range of play places are possible when compared to homes in commercial areas. In the former, places available might be gardens, pavements, landscaped areas and wild places; in the latter, streets, car parks, shopping precincts and parks could be used. There will be many places in common to both areas but certain that will be unavailable to children in the alternative location. This will necessarily affect the range of possible play activities for the children from the different areas.

A related issue here is that of local child-density. Rural children and those in low child density areas may have some distance to travel to play with friends. They may be denied the level of social play that they desire, and will be unable to play games involving a large number of players.

A child whose local landscape is flat has greater potential for moving around, both for meeting other children and also for using a wider range of outdoor play places than a child living in a hilly area. Here, outdoor play patterns can be severely constrained both by the more difficult travelling and also by the lack of flat play spaces (Berg and Medrich 1980).

In a similar way to hills, major roads can seriously curtail the number of outdoor places available for play. Heavy traffic on local streets may lead to them being forbidden children as play places.

Child factors

The concept of "home range" is useful in understanding how standard child factors such as age and sex affect a child's possible use of the outdoor environment. A consideration of a child's home range together with the environmental constraints outlined in the previous section, will give a good picture of the opportunities available to a given child in a given setting.

1. The concept of home range.   Home range (or territorial range) indicates "the spatial extent and experiential variety of outdoor places inhabited. It embraces the totality of a child's space-time domain of familiar places close to home as well as a constantly expanding boundary condition, leading to unfamiliar challenging encounters in new places" (Moore and Young 1978).

Home range is a dynamic phenomenon which develops and extends as the child interacts with its environment. The child seeks to extend its range in order to encompass new destinations with their associated novelty. Range extension is a discontinuous process, with large increases in range associated with events such as starting school or riding a bike. The development of the range is a more continuous process, as the child explores and transforms its territory over time. Natural places within the home range are a prime source of change and variety, providing children with settings that allow continual monitoring and interest.

Moore and Young (1978) suggest three levels at which children may be involved with their territorial range. "Habitual range" represents close to home activities. It develops during the pre-school years starting with the private spaces immediately around the home, and then extending into the nearby public domain of local streets, playgrounds and wasteground. "Frequented range" incorporates those places visited perhaps at weekends or during holidays in a regular way. "Occasional range" relates to exotic places visited only rarely and under unusual circumstances. It is the habitual range of children that is the most important and interesting, especially in the study of younger children, whose play is almost totally restricted to places near to home and within the habitual range.

2. Age and home range.   It is common observation that younger children have smaller home ranges than do older ones. This has been empirically demonstrated in an American study by Coates and Bussard (1974). They investigated the patterns of spatial behaviour of 35 children on a moderate density housing development. The patterns varied consistently with age and so the findings were grouped for the ages 4–5 years, 6–9 years and 10–12 years. The home range of the youngest group was in the form of a compact home-based hubble, extending about 50 ft from the front doors with lateral expansion to a boundary of about 90–140 ft. This covered public and private family zones, and those public areas within sight. The range of 6 to 9 year olds had expanded in area by a factor of 10 and in path length by a factor of 5 to 8. This meant fuller access to a larger range of public and private places including friends' houses and more playgrounds. By 10–12 years, the home range encompassed both a considerable range of local habitual places, together with a large number of places further afield including wild areas.

3. Sex and home range.   With younger children up to 5 years old, Coates and Bussard (op.cit.) found that the restrictions on home range were comparable between the sexes. However with 6–9 year olds, the boys had a larger home range. Almost all the girls' friends lived within the same or adjacent cul-de-sac, whereas the boys' friends were spread further afield. Boys used unowned areas more than girls, and girls were chaperoned to more places than were boys. For 10–12 year olds the trends continued with girls having to use safer areas such as playgrounds for play whereas boys went more often to wild areas and other "risky" places.

4. Parental attitudes and home range.   These change both with the age and sex of the child and may be largely responsible for the age/sex differences in home range scale. Parents of younger children in Coates and Bussard's study required them to be in view and with easy access to the house, and there were firm boundaries to where the child might go. The 6–9 year olds were accorded more freedom to move further afield, often having to ask permission first. This was particularly true for girls with whom parents were stricter. Similar trends applied to the oldest age-group with parents continuing to be stricter with girls. There were individual differences between parents of children of comparable age and sex.

Parent's fear for their children's safety is a major factor in influencing where children are allowed to play. In a study by Berg and Medrich (1980), traffic safety was a major parental concern. Judgement by the parents as to whether their children could or could not cross busy roads or play near traffic hazards affected the extent of children's home range. The personal safety of the child was also a concern with children being forbidden places where they might be harassed or those considered to be physically dangerous e.g. derelict buildings. Parents were more likely to agree to hazards being negotiated if the child was either older or a boy.

WHICH OUTDOOR ENVIRONMENT?

Having discussed why and when children may choose to play outdoors, and looked at the factors constraining the range of places available to them, we can now turn to consideration of which outdoor environments the children actually choose to play in.

An early study by Hole (1966) looked at the use, for play, of the spaces round 12 British inner-city housing estates. Play was located primarily on paved areas, then playgrounds and then in the access areas to the dwellings. Kinds of play observed were "street games" such as chase, catch, skipping etc., play with wheeled vehicles, physical play such as climbing, swinging etc. and also a lot of social interaction. The low usage of grassed areas for play was felt to be a reflection of management policy rather than of low popularity with the children. Although the playgrounds often served as foci for the children's play, they failed to divert children away from playing on roads and paved areas when they required hard surfaces for wheeled vehicles and roller skates. There was no suitable space on the playgrounds themselves for this activity. Children spent only a very short time in the playgrounds, an average of only 14.5 minutes.

A number of American studies observing children at play in different local environments have extended these early results. Similar preferences for paved areas and for playgrounds can still be seen.

In a study evaluating the use of an inner city residential area in Baltimore for recreation, Brower and Williamson (1974) described how children used the streets and alleys as play places, and also the provided playgrounds. Here, parents' fear for the safety of the children was a major determining factor in the use of sites.

Children's play in a low-rise inner-city housing development in San Francisco was investigated by Cooper Marcus (1974). The development had specially designed and landscaped interior courtyards with play facilities. They were away from the traffic and sheltered from the wind. Play indeed took place predominantly in these places rather than on pavements or roadsides which were also available. Marcus felt that the attraction of the courtyards was due to a combination of factors: the wind shelter, the sense of territory created by living rooms overlooking the courtyards (very good for the supervision of young children), the presence of play equipment indicating that play is "expected to take place there", the landscaping and the inclusion of vertical elements e.g. fences, trees, platforms. Hard surface play was catered for in these interior spaces so the children were not forced to seek opportunities elsewhere.

A further study on play opportunities in the urban environment compared the effect of four different local environments on children's play patterns (Berg and Medrich 1980). The four neighbourhoods differed in social status, terrain and levels of access to planned and unplanned play space. Although each had some amount of organised play space, children were not always attracted to it, through either the distance, the traffic or the threat of "older people". Instead, unplanned "found" play spaces were highly prized e.g. waste ground, untidy streams, and also the streets:

"Despite apparent danger, however, the children found the streets generally more exciting than a myriad of other play spaces. Parks and playgrounds (planned with children in mind) were often seen as dull in comparison with interesting street life." (Berg and Medrich 1980, p. 341). The attractiveness of the streets for play and the enormous variety of activities taking place there have been extensively documented by the Opie's (1969).

Play activities in a suburban residential area in New England were described by Aiello, Gordon and Farrell (1974). The study area had no playground and "the children lamented the lack of one". The environment most used by the children outdoors was the streets, but natural areas including trees, streams, ponds and shrub areas were also popular. "Natural areas seem to be valuable to children as places for learning about parts of natural systems and as places where certain activities such as exploring, digging or climbing are better accommodated than in other of the suburban developments. "(Aiello et al., op. cit., p. 195). Again, parents attitudes as to whether such areas were safe for play or not considerably affected the level of their use. The most commonly observed activities were wheeled vehicle related, then standing around or walking, then playing with balls, sports, swinging, chatting and playing with water.

In his in-depth study of children's use of the spaces around a complete New England town, Hart (1979) catalogued a whole range of places which were used for play. Children played round their houses, tending to play at the front or sides of the house rather than at the rear. This allowed them to see what other people were doing, and to be seen themselves, in order to attract other children to their play. Small patches of soil (dirt) were the most intensively used of all places, where mock highway systems and houses could be built. Children spent a lot of time building places for themselves, mostly within 100 yards of their houses. This occurred because of the availability of non-adult claimed areas nearby, and because of the presence of flexible landscape elements and loose parts for building. Children also spent a lot of time alone in quiet pastimes e.g. dabbling in water. The rivers and lakes were the most highly valued places although not all were in the range of the children. Woods, trees, brooks and small "frog ponds" were also high on children's lists of preferred places.

Similar preferences for natural places were shown by rural English children interviewed by Humberside Playing Fields Association (1982). Children played on patches of wasteland, corners of fields and bits of woodland "with such delights as mud hills, tarzan swings, becks, bumpy tracks and bushes for hiding in" (p. 2). Of the children spoken to, 71% used their local play area to some extent, although some did not go there at all because they found it boring. When asked what they would like in their ideal play area, both sexes strongly desired trees for climbing, also shrubs, bushes and bumpy ground for hiding/ fantasy games.

In summary, children are necessarily limited by the available opportunities with their accessible environment. However within this range of possible places certain kinds of places and environmental attributes are seemingly preferred over others.

The range of possible environments is perhaps most limited for inner-city children. If playgrounds here are attractive and well sited, then they will be used, being one of few places where children are allowed or expected to play (Cooper Marcus 1974). If not, then children will play in what may be the only alternative places, on the streets and pavements. These may be more attractive in many ways such as socially and for their hard surfaces. In suburban areas children have a greater likelihood of being able to play in a garden and have fewer restrictions from traffic. They may or may not have access to a playground. They are more likely to play in natural rather than man-made places than are inner-city children. Both suburban and rural children prize the trees, woods and streams available to them as play places even though they may only have access to them infrequently. Playgrounds here may be welcome as social foci for the area providing a known meeting point for kids.

As playgrounds or designated play spaces seem to be the inevitable (though not necessarily the correct or most appropriate) planning solution to improving children's play facilities, it is worth considering in more detail the kind of provision that should be made.

WHAT KIND OF PLAYGROUND?

Traditional playgrounds with swings, slides and "Jungle Gyms" (climbing frames) often set in tarmac, hold children's interest for only a brief period (Hole 1966). A study of traditional playgrounds in England by Holme and Massie (1971) compared the possible number of users in a playgrounds catchment area to the numbers actually using it, finding proportions as low as 3%. The low use of these traditional facilities and children's preference for other environments such as the streets or woods, has led designers to experiment with new structures and new kinds of playgrounds. These are as alternatives to the readymade standard items found in manufacturer's catalogues.

One alternative style of playground originally pioneered in England by Marjorie Allen in her book "Planning for Play" (1968), is the adventure playground. Her book illustrates a number of different designs, including some by Arvid Bengtsson a leadng playground designer (Bengtsson 1970). In an adventure playground there are very few fixed facilities—perhaps a small building for quiet activities and the play leader's office. The majority of elements are loose and arranged by the children as they create their own play structures. The building of these various enterprises by the children themselves is part of the intended play activities at the playground, because they can stimulate a wide range of beneficial physical and social activities. Spivak (1970) describes how a traditional playground, heavily subjected to vandalism, was turned into an adventure playground with the help of the local children. It proved to be very popular and also to have low rates of vandalism.

The relative attractiveness to children of adventure playgrounds over other sorts has been demonstrated in work by Hayward, Rothenburg and Beasley (1974). At three sorts of playgrounds, adventure, traditional and contemporary (wooden bars, nets etc.) measures of attendance and ranges of activities were recorded. The adventure playground was not only the most popular but also had the greatest variety of play activities associated with it. However, as the populations of children were different at the different playgrounds, these results are not as strong as they might be.

Moore's (1974) in-depth study of an adventure playground showed how varied were the patterns of creative activities. He distinguished two main dimensions on which activities could be placed: degree of mobility (focus→chain→flow), or size of territorial range (concentrated→contained→expansive). In

these terms activity at a traditional playground would character-
istically be of low mobility (focus) with small territorial range
(concentrated/contained). Moore particularly stressed the importance of the interaction of loose and fixed elements in
providing the wide range of play activities.

Because adventure playgrounds allow or encourage this wide
range of activities, it is thought that their use is of particular
importance to handicapped children. They especially need
opportunities and stimulation to try out and develop a wide
range of skills. A study by Wolff (1979) compared the kinds of
activities in which blind children participated at both adventure
and traditional playgrounds. The largest proportions of both
social interaction and solitary play were observed at the
adventure playground. Wolff suggests that these two play types
are the most important for child development, fostering
qualities of initiative and independence as well as social
know-how.

Unfortunately, adventure playgrounds may not be provided
for a number of reasons. Firstly, objections from local residents,
that they are noisy, untidy and dangerous. Secondly the local
councils may object to the recurring annual costs of staff and
materials in contrast to the (supposed) one-off cost of a fixed
playground. In England, many of the London authorities and
some of the New Towns run adventure playgrounds, but on the
whole the trend is still to provide fixed equipment sites whenever
a new playground is required. Play provision and its funding can
be a highly political area as it is often in competition with other
worthwhile causes for money. As the current trend is still
towards fixed playgrounds for the reasons discussed, it becomes
necessary to assess the importance and value for play of
individual items of play equipment with which these fixed sites
will be stocked, whilst acknowledging that the ideal playground
would have very little fixed equipment.

CHOICE OF PLAY EQUIPMENT

It is very difficult to assess the play "value" of play equipment. If we take an evolutionary view of play such as that of Bruner (1976), then play has become "built in" to our way of life because its benefits to us have outweighed its costs. "Good" play equipment should then offer a lot to each child for negligible cost. However it is very difficult to decide a priori what *kinds* of play an item of equipment should allow, and how much, before it is classed as "good". Should it provide a setting for social or physical play, and which is more important? Is a piece which allows a range of physical activities better than one which constrains children to just one? Who decides what "good" means?

One answer is to take children's judgement on whether play equipment is "good" or not, especially as they are the definitive users. The simplest measures of their feelings about items are whether they use them or not, and for how long. Similarly, the kinds of play activities offered by equipment can only be realistically assessed by observing what happens on individual pieces rather than taking manufacturers' descriptions of what *should* happen on it. For these reasons I carried out detailed observations of children at play in three local playgrounds in the south of England (Naylor 1982). I suggested that "good" play equipment would be items offering both a range of kinds of play (e.g. social and physical), and also a range of activities within each kind of play. This was reasoned from a consideration of the number and range of opportunities presented to the child for new learning, experimentation and practice.

Unfortunately, children's use of the equipment did not reflect the range of play forms associated with individual items as predicted. Perhaps if there had been a greater overall range of kinds of play instead of the predominantly physical play observed, then a different relationship would have been found.

However, a consistent preference for items across all three playgrounds was found in terms of their modal physical activity: sliding items were used most, then swings and then climbing items. However, certain items which combined social play with physical play were also popular even above slides and swings. A wooden fort which was used for climbing, as a social centre and as a setting for fantasy play was the most popular item at one playground, even though it did not involve the vertiginous sensations associated with slides, swings and roundabouts. Another popular piece also involved considerable social play in its use. This was a suspended cable with a sliding pulley system where children spent more time negotiating with partners for co-operation to use it than they did actually sliding. Both the fort and the pulley system were recent additions to their playgrounds, and therefore novel, and this no doubt added to their attractiveness.

There were consistent age differences across all three sites between young children up to 5 years, and school age children. Not only were the younger group more likely to be accompanied by their mothers, they interacted less with other children and chose to play on different kinds of equipment. They generally favoured small scale items such as rocking animals, small climbers, tunnels and wendy houses. They used smaller versions of standard items e.g. cradle swings if provided. If there were only a few items of appropriate size for younger children, then they had either little range of opportunities or else were tempted into playing on items which required greater competence and strength than they perhaps possessed.

This returns us to the question of safety addressed earlier, as young children using equipment designed for older ones can experience severe hazards, e.g. not having sufficient reach to cross gaps, insufficient strength to hold on to roundabouts, fear of heights etc. Manufacturers have concentrated on the safety aspect of equipment as a selling point, as this has been easier to articulate than the play value of their wares. The main emphasis has been on the structural safety of items, that they have adequate strengths and tolerances and that they won't rust. It is quite obvious however, from informal observation, that a structurally sound time can still give rise to accidents. This may be because the actions carried out by children on the equipment have not been envisaged by the designer. For example, children run up slides as well as sliding down so that on a free-standing slide, off-ground collisions are possible. Similarly on swings, once children are bored with the normal method of swinging, they may try kneeling on the swing, shortening the swing chains or even climbing on the frame, all sources of increased risk. It is important that equipment is assessed for safety in terms of how it may be used as well as in terms of its material structure.

CONCLUSIONS AND RECOMMENDATIONS

Any study of children's play is incomplete without a consideration of the setting for that play. Whilst it is true that a child can play anywhere, the studies reviewed here indicate the extent to which the content of the outdoor environment can limit children's outdoor play. Local environments will vary both physically and socially. Space size, availability, nearness, surfacing and the facilities therein, whether play equipment or loose elements or vegetation, will all vary from one home location to another. Similarly the number of friends and ease of access to them will vary between residential districts. Whilst few play activities will actually be excluded as a result of these differences, it becomes more likely that certain play styles will be found in one place rather than another.

Children need and will use spaces that are set aside for their play. If these do not exist, then they will necessarily use non-designated areas e.g. streets, wasteground etc. This is also true if the designated areas do not match the needs of the children, perhaps for hard surfaces, loose elements for building or just for novelty and change. It is not necessarily the case that the spaces set aside for play should be playgrounds per se. The decision on what to provide for children should be based on a full consideration of the existing and lacking facilities in their local environment. The play needs of inner-city and suburban children are quite different, yet often met by exactly the same "playground" solution, even to the items included. It might be more appropriate to provide city children with access to "wild" natural areas and water, and to provide social facilities for suburban kids.

Whatever provision is made, it must be within the home range of the children and agreeable to the parents. Pre-school children need to play close to parents or to supervising adults and yet to have contact with children of their own age. They need to be able to manipulate and to explore the environment, to play with a wide range of toys, to run and make noise, to use up energy, stretch their muscles and so forth. Children this age in single family houses are usually adequately provided for, but those in high rise developments may well have severe limitations to their play space. School-age children need opportunities close to home for motor development (climbing, running, swinging etc.), for social play, ball games, fantasy, bicycling and making noise. They are not limited to the areas adjacent to their homes in finding appropriate spaces for these activities, but their demands on the environment are greater and more complex.

If a playground is to be provided for children, then the most popular and successful ones are adventure playgrounds. They provide children with a range of materials and opportunities, and allow them to construct their own play environment. Despite their obvious popularity and benefit to children, they are rarely provided by the authorities. Instead fixed playgrounds are built. Of the items generally included in such sites, slides, swings and then climbing frames are the most popular. However certain items favouring social play as well as physical are also popular particularly if they are novel to the children. It is still not possible to decide in advance just what will be a good piece of play equipment. Although manufacturers try to ensure the structural safety of their products, insufficient thought has been given to the way in which children will explore all possibilities of an item, including possibly risky activities. Young children are often under provided for within playgrounds as they need smaller scale items than do school-age children. Also they can be at risk from using equipment that is designed for older children with their greater strength and skill. All these factors should be taken into account when planning a playground.

Although children's play has been very much a minority concern in the past, it is now becoming a national issue with the recent designation of a Minister for Play in Britain. A national Association for Children's Play and Recreation has recently been formed with funding for provision and research. Hopefully these are encouraging signs that children are being borne in mind more, when adults are planning the environments in which both they have to live and children have to play.

References

Aiello, J.F., Gordon, B. and Farrell, T.J. (1974). Description of children's outdoor activities in a suburban residential area: Preliminary findings. In R.C. Moore (Ed.), *Childhood city man-environment interactions.* Vol. 12. D. Carson (general Ed.). Milwaukee: EDRA. pp. 187–195.

Allen, M. (1968). *Planning for play.* London: Thames and Hudson.

Baker, D. (1977). Worlds of play. *Childhood education,* **53**, 245–249.

Barker, R.G. and Wright, H.F. (1955). *Midwest and its children.* White Plains, New York: Row, Peterson and Company.

Bengtsson, A. (1970). Environmental planning for children's play. New York: Praeger.

Berg, M. and Medrich, E.A. (1980). The physical environment and its effect on play and play patterns. *Environment and behavior*, **12**, 320–348.

Brower, S.N. and Williamson, P. (1974). Outdoor recreation as a function of the urban housing environment. *Environment and behavior*, **6**, 295–345.

Bruner, J.S. (1976). Nature and uses of immaturity. In J.S. Bruner, A. Jolly, and K. Sylva, (Eds.), *Play—Its role in development and evolution*. New York: Penguin Books.

Coates, G. and Bussard, E. (1974). Patterns of children's spatial behaviour in a moderate density housing development. In R.C. Moore (Ed.), *Childhood city man-environment interactions*. Vol. 12. D. Carson (general Ed.). Milwaukee: EDRA. 131–141.

Cooper Marcus, C. (1974). Children's play behavior in a low-rise, inner-city housing development. In R.C. Moore (Ed.), *Childhood city man-environment interactions*. Vol. 12. D. Carson (general Ed.). Milwaukee: EDRA. 197–211.

Department of Environment (1973). *Children at play*. London: HMSO, Design Bulletin 27.

Gehlbach, R.D. (1980). Instructional play: some theoretical prerequisites to systematic research and development. *Educational psychologist*, **15**, 112–124.

Hart, R. (1979). *Children's experience of place: A developmental study*. New York: Irvington Press.

Hayward, D.G., Rothenburg, M., and Beasley, R.R. (1974). Children's play and urban playground environments: A comparison of traditional, contemporary and adventure playground types. *Environment and behavior*, **6**, 131–168.

Hole, V. (1966). *Children's play on housing estates*. National Building Studies Research Paper 39. London: HMSO.

Holme, A. and Massie, D. (1971). *Children's play: A study of needs and opportunities*. London: Michael Joseph.

Humberside Playing Fields Association (1982). *Where we play*. Available from HPFA, 14, Market Place, Howden, Goole, North Humberside DN 14 7BJ, U.K.

Kaplan, S. (1977). Tranquillity and challenge in the natural environment. In *Children nature and the urban environment: Proceedings of a symposium fair*. USDA Forest Service paper, USDA FSGTR NE-30. Washington DC: US Government Printing Office. pp. 181–186.

Moore, R. (1974). Patterns of activity in time and space: The ecology of a neighbourhood playground. In D.V. Canter and T.R. Lee (Eds.), *Psychology and the built environment*. London: Architectural Press.

Moore, R. and Young, D. (1978). Childhood outdoors: Toward a social ecology of the landscape. In I. Altman and J.F. Wohlwill (Eds.), *Children and the environment*, Vol. 3. *Human behavior and environment*. New York: Plenum Press. 83–130.

Naylor, H.V. (1982). *Design for outdoor play: An observational study*. Unpublished M.Sc. thesis, University of Surrey, Guildford.

Opie, I. and Opie, P. (1969). *Children's games in street and playground*. Oxford: Clarendon Press.

Shafer, E.L. (1977). Research needs for programs that provide natural environments for children. In *Children nature and the urban environment: Proceedings of a symposium fair*. USDA Forest Service paper, USDA FSGTR NE-30. Washington DC: US Government Printing Office. pp. 215–218.

Spivak, M. (1970). The political collapse of a playground. *Landscape architecture*, **59**, 288–291.

Wolff, P.M. (1979). The adventure playground as a therapeutic environment. In D. Canter and S. Canter (Eds.), *Designing for therapeutic environments: A review of research*. Chichester: Wiley.

Notes on contributors

LARRY FENSON

Larry Fenson is at the Developmental Psychology Laboratory, College of Science, San Diego State University, San Diego, CA 92182, U.S.A.

ROBERT E. SCHELL

Robert E. Schell is a science writer and author of *Developmental psychology today*.

PETER K. SMITH

Peter K. Smith is at the Department of Psychology, University of Sheffield, S10 2TN, U.K. He is editor of *Play in animals and humans* (1984).

MEHRI TAKHVAR and NEIL GORE

Mehri Takhvar and Neil Gore are at the Department of Psychology, University of Sheffield, Sheffield S10 2TN, U.K.

RALPH VOLLSTEDT

Ralph Vollstedt is at the Psykologisk Laboratorium, Kobenhavns Universitet, Amager, Njalsgade 94, 2300 Kobenhavn S, Denmark.

JAMES F. CHRISTIE

James F. Christie is at the Department of Curriculum and Instruction. University of Kansas, Lawrence, Kansas 66044, U.S.A.

STAN A. KUCZAJ

Stan A. Kuczaj II is at the Department of Psychology, Southern Methodist University, Dallas, Texas 75275, U.S.A.

TONY SIMON

Tony Simon is now at the School of Psychology, Lancashire Polytechnic, Preston PR1 2TQ, U.K.

ROY McCONKEY

Roy McConkey is at St Michael's House, Upper Kilmacud Road, Stillorgan, Co. Dublin, Eire.

CHARLES R. SCHAEFER

Charles E. Schaefer is at The Children's Village, Dobbs Ferry, New York 10522, U.S.A. He is editor of the *Handbook of play therapy* (1983).

HEATHER NAYLOR

Heather Naylor is now at Logica, 64 Newman Street, London W1A 4SE, U.K.

Author Index

147

Subject Index

151